TOURISM IN THE ECONOMY OF MADHYA PRADESH

TOURISM IN THE ECONOMY OF MADHYA PRADESH

RAJIV DUBE

1987

DAYA PUBLISHING HOUSE

DELHI-110006

ISBN 81-7035-029-8

Published by Anil Mittal for Daya Publishing House at 1302, Vaid Wara, Nai Sarak, Delhi-110006. Phone: 260116
Printed at H.K. Printers, Delhi.

PRINTED IN INDIA

Preface

Tourism as an economic activity is difficult to measure and analyse. But, whenever the development of tourism is considered and promotional efforts are introduced—in particular by developing countries—it is mostly because of the contribution that tourism is expected to make to national economic growth. It is rightly felt that a competitive tourist industry opens up chances to earn foreign exchange and, besides its effect on the balance of payments, tourism undoubtedly creates additional employment and rising incomes. Tourism may also contribute to better income distribution.

The present study is an attempt to evaluate the role of tourism in the State economy. No comprehensive systematic studies relating to the contribution of tourism, to the economy of the State, were made earlier. Therefore, this study can prove to be helpful in determining the extent and role of tourism in the State economy. It is also interesting to note that no reliable data are available regarding employment and other financial aspects before 1980 for the tourist sector in the official records. That is why, in the present study, the statistical information collected for analysis, from sixteen major tourist centres and other private and official sources, has been since 1980.

The present work is broadly arranged under six chapters.

The first chapter deals with the theoretical orientation. It deals with the nature and role of tourism in the national economy, some economic implications of tourism, the main features of the tourist industry, and the development of tourism in the different plan periods at the national level. In short, this chapter depicts the place of tourism at the national level.

The second chapter is a survey of available literature and also presents the research methodology which has been adopted for data processing, tabulation and analysis.

The third chapter deals with the importance of tourism in the regional economy of Madhya Pradesh. For this purpose, different models have been constructed to show the impact of external factors or 'E', like tourism, on the State economy or 'a'. The progress and development of tourism in the state plan periods has also been included in this chapter. Besides this, tourist places of Madhya Pradesh and the organization of tourism have been briefly described.

The fourth chapter is significant from the point of view of the study. It presents the structure of employment that can be made available through the tourist industry in the State. A complete study of the employment potential of tourism in the State has been made, the results have been tabulated and systematically presented purely on the basis of the survey reports and other publications.

The fifth chapter deals with the financial aspects, relating to expenditure and revenue, and presents the budgetary provision for this sector of the economy.

In the last chapter, conclusions have been drawn on the basis of the analysis of data. In the light of the present investigation, a few suggestions have been made for improving the existing situation of the tourism in the State.

I take this opportunity to express my deep sense of indebtedness to Professor V.P. Pande, (M.Com., Ph.D. London and Sagar), Retired Professor and Head, Department of Economics, Doctor Harisingh Gour Vishwavidyalaya, Sagar (M.P.), for his valuable guidance and untiring interest during the pursuit of this investigation.

I wish to record my sincere thanks to Dr A. Raman, (M.A., B.L., Ph.D.), Head, Department of Economics, Doctor Harisingh Gour Vishwavidyalaya, Sagar (M.P.) and to other staff members of the Department for their constant encouragement and inspiration.

My thanks are due also to Professor S. Mallikarjunan, Retired Professor and Head, Department of English, Doctor Harisingh Gour Vishwavidyalaya, Sagar, for looking through the manuscript.

I am extremely grateful to the authorities of the University Grants Commission, New Delhi, for awarding me a Junior Research Fellowship, which gave me the financial support as well as an opportunity to continue my work on this subject, and I would also like to thank the authorities of the Jawaharlal Nehru University Library, Sagar Tourist Bunglow, Sagar; India Tourism Development Corporation Library, New Delhi; Indian Council of World Affairs Library, Sapru House, New Delhi; Directorate of Tourism, Government of Madhya Pradesh, Bhopal; Prachiya Niketan, Bhopal; Madhya Pradesh State Tourism Development Corporation, Bhopal; Directorate of Economics and Statistics, Madhya Pradesh, Bhopal and Sardar Patel Institute of Economic and Social Research, Ahmedabad, for extending help in collecting the required material for my research work.

I am thankful to Dr M.N. Limaye, Department of Public Administration, Doctor Harisingh Gour Vishwavidyalaya, Sagar and Shri A.K. Ray, Managing Director, Madhya Pradesh Tourism Development Corporation, Bhopal, for their generous co-operation given to me.

I would be failing in my duty if I do not express my heartful veneration and gratitude for my respected parents, and sisters for their inspiration and encouragement and their sacrifices, which have enabled me to pursue my studies.

Last, but not the least, I am thankful to Shri Shoukat Ali for his neat and efficient typing of the manuscript.

RAJIV DUBE

Contents

1

Tourism in the National Economy

Tourism is a powerful instrument for gratifying man's most compelling desires of experiencing the sweet and virginal grandeur of nature, of broadening the vision and deepening his understanding of diverse cultures and civilizations. A peculiar characteristic of tourism is that it is a highly technical and specialized branch in which a rational coordination of private and public sectors, together with continuous stimulus from government, is extremely essential. Unlike any other industry, it offers greater scope for economic, social, cultural and regional development programmes of some countries. In the developing countries as well as in the developed nations, tourism has opened new areas for economic advancement, without exporting anything except ideas: the idea of shopping; the idea of variety; the idea of a holiday in the sun. Therefore, it is known as 'an industry without chimneys' or 'a smokeless industry'.

ECONOMIC SIGNIFICANCE OF TOURISM

Unprecedented economic prosperity in many parts of the globe together with greater leisure and the revolutionary growth of air transportation have put tourism at the top of international business today. In recent times, the Governments of developing countries have begun devoting attention to the promotion of tourism through an integrated approach. In these countries, tourism has come to be recognised as an industry, providing employment opportunities and generating economic growth, besides earning foreign exchange. The following are some economic implications of tourism.

1. Tourism as a Creator of Jobs

The tourist industry is a 'labour-intensive service industry' and hence is a valuable source of employment. In many of the developing countries, where chronic unemployment and disguised employment often exists, the promotion of tourism can prove to be an encouragement to economic development and, especially, employment. "Tourism as a source of employment", says Medlik, "is particularly important for areas with limited alternative sources of employment, as is often the case in non-industrial areas deficient in natural resources other than scenic attractions and climate."[1] Millions of people throughout the world now depend for their employment on tourism. It employs large numbers of people and provides a wide range of jobs which extends from the unskilled to the highly specialised. Some are directly involved in the tourism plant like the hotels, motels, air-transport, railways and other services directly used by the tourists; and others are indirectly involved, such as, in the entertainment industry, souvenir, trade, etc. A survey conducted by the National Council of Applied Economic Research (NCAER), New Delhi, in 1975, estimated that about 9,33,000 persons were directly or indirectly employed in the tourist industry.[2] Presently the Tata Economic and Consultancy Services Limited, Bombay, is conducting a survey on behalf of the Department of Tourism on this aspect of the tourism industry. On the basis of the growth in tourism over the past six years, this figure can be roughly estimated at 2.0 millions.[3] Moreover tourism is also responsible for creating employment outside the industry in its narrowly defined sense and in this context McIntosh said, "It scores noticeably over other forms of new industry."[4] Those who supply goods and services, to those induced employment includes, for example, those involved in the construction industry, in furnishing and equipment industries, and in farming and food supply. It is interesting that the tourist industry is one of the few in which more women are employed than men in many countries.

According to an estimate about 1,40,000 persons are directly employed in the tourist industry in Switzerland and about a million persons in the United Kingdom. In the U.S., for every 1,000 guests in hotels, the total jobs created are 386 in the hotel and ancillary industries.[5]

It is estimated that 54 per cent of expenditure by tourist is accounted for by the wages and salaries of the personnel in the tourist industry. One room in a hotel is estimated to create three direct and nine indirect jobs. The raising of hotel accommodation to about 40,000 rooms by 1982 alone, thus, can create nearly 70,000 direct jobs and over 2,00,000 indirect jobs and that too for the local people.[6]

In many tourist areas, the working population employment is of a seasonal nature only. This is especially true of 'marginal' areas where, there are also few possibilities of alternative out-of-season employment. Strenuous efforts are for this reason being made to lengthen the season by such attractions as illuminations, festivals and reduced prices for out-of-season holiday making. "Thus tourism can be an essential feature of regional economic development at least in respect of creating work."[7]

2. The Multiplier Effect

The tourist multiplier is an attempt to go behind tourist receipts, and find out the expenditure profile of the tourists, the nature of their preferences and the volume of their transactions. The multiplier effect of tourist expenditure on the economy of the destination country is well known, whereby every unit of money spent on tourism circulates in the economy, and brings about an increased area of benefit to the people concerned. Tourist expenditure supports not only the tourist industry directly but helps indirectly to support numerous other industries which supply goods and services to the tourist industry. In this way, money spent by the tourist, may be said to be used several times and spreads into various sectors of the economy. Every time the money changes hands it provides 'new' income, and the continuing series of conversions of the money spent by the tourist forms what the economist terms 'the multiplier effect'. The more times the conversion occurs, the greater is its beneficial effect on the

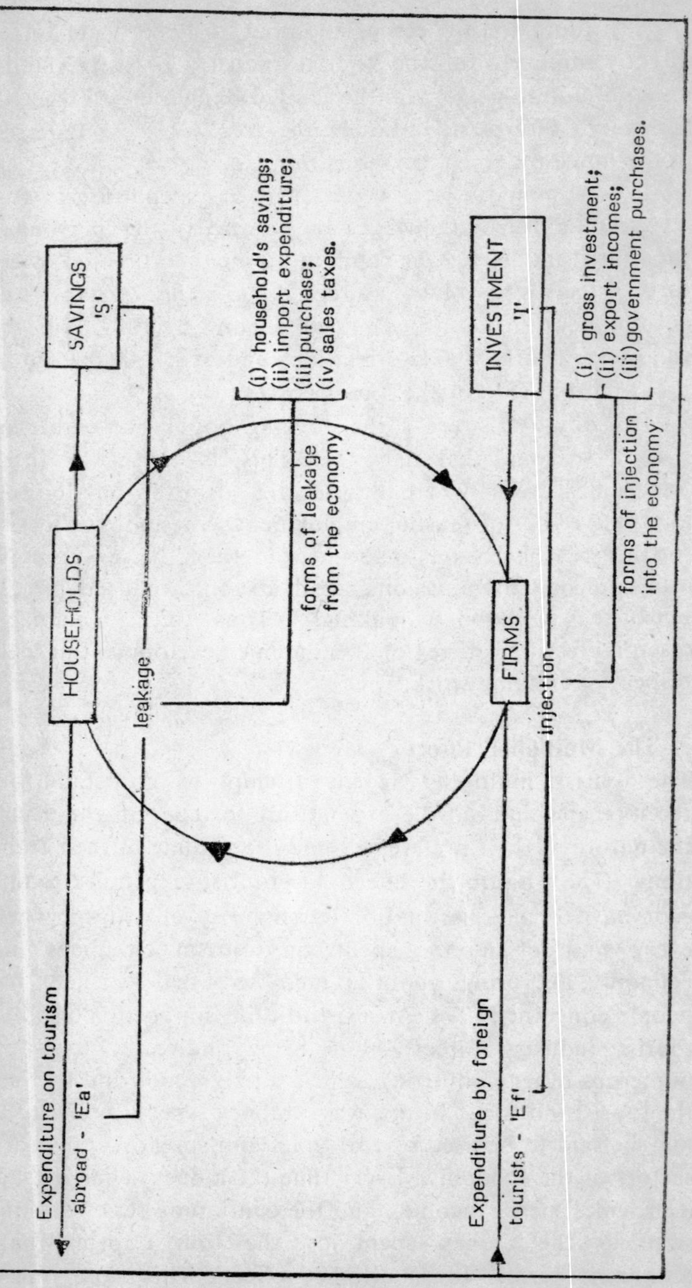

Fig. 1.1: CIRCULAR FLOW OF MONEY

economy. However, this transfer of money cannot go on indefinitely because of, 'leakages' which occur. Such leakages may consist of, for instance, imported foreign goods, interest on foreign investments, or savings which withdraw money from circulation, and any leakages of these kinds will reduce the stream of expenditure which in consequence will limit and reduce the multiplier effect.

A model can be made based on the circular flow of money in the economy (with reference to tourism) (Fig. 1.1). It illustrates that the households' savings, import expenditure, purchases and sales taxes are examples of withdrawals of money from the circular flow; gross investments, export incomes and government purchases on the other hand are additions to the circular flow of money. Whereas expenditure on tourism abroad represents a 'leakage' in the national economy, expenditures by foreign tourists from an invisible export and so represents an 'injection' into the economy.

The calculation of the tourism multiplier, however, is by no means easy and such estimates as have been made in the case of a number of economies show very wide variations.[8] Table 1.1 shows the tourist multiplier in the various countries.

TABLE 1.1: **Estimated Tourist Multiplier**

Sl. No.	*Country*	*Multiplier Value*
1.	Pacific and the Far East	3.2—4.3[9]
2.	New Hampshire	1.6—1.7[10]
3.	Hawaii	0.9—1.3[11]
4.	Greece	1.2—1.4[12]
5.	Pakistan	3.3[13]
6.	Ireland	2.7[14]
7.	Lebanon	1.2—1.4[15]
8.	Bahamas	1.36[16]
9.	The United Kingdom	2.95[17]
10.	India	3.2—3.6[18]

Peters expresses the opinion that in these particular studies some of the multipliers were too high (as in the case of the Far East, Pakistan and Ireland) while others were probably much too conservative (as in the case of Hawaii, Greece and Lebanon).[19] It may be added that according to the Zinder Report, the comparable multiplier effect of the tourist spending is 8.4 in Yugoslavia and 3.2 in South East Asia.[20]

The tourist multiplier is based upon some unrealistic assumption like constant ratios of propensity to import and consume, taxation to income and factor income shares to the national income. In addition, the chain effects are measured only upto the first or second round of expenditure. The ME (multiplier effect) on tourist car agencies, owners of antique-shops, tailors and other recipients is quite indeterminate. Nevertheless, a simple Keynesian model is presented below.

In an open Keynesian economy, the basic equation of the general multiplier can be drawn as following:[21]

$$S+E_a=I+E_f \qquad \text{———————}(1)$$

where, $S+E_a$ represent 'leakages' from the tourists' home country in the shape of savings and expenditure on tourism abroad; and

$I+E_f$ represent 'injections' of investment and expenditure by foreign tourists in the nation visited.

It is assumed the S and E_a vary solely with households' income within a relatively narrow price range of services. Thus

$$S=f_1\ (Y) \qquad \text{———————}(2)$$

$$E_a=f_2\ (Y) \qquad \text{———————}(3)$$

Further $\triangle S=s\triangle Y$ and $\triangle E_a=e_a\triangle Y$.

These equations mean that households vary savings by a constant fraction of the income, S and expenditure on tourism by a constant fraction, e_a', in response to a change in income.

From the equilibrium condition of (1) we get

$$\triangle S+\triangle E_a=\triangle I+\triangle E_f \qquad \text{———}(4)$$

From (2), (3), and (4) we get

$$S\triangle Y+e_a\triangle Y=\triangle I+\triangle E_f$$

so that

$$Y = \frac{1}{s + e_a} (I + E_f) \qquad \text{———————(5)}$$

Thus, the change in income will be Kt times the change in investment or expenditure by foreign tourists, where Kt is equal to reciprocal of the marginal propensity to save plus the marginal propensity to spend abroad. If 25 per cent of an increment in income is saved and 15 per cent spent on tourism, then s is .25 and e_a is .15.

Hence $$Kt = \frac{1}{.25 + .15} = 2.5$$

A change in I or E_f will lead to an increase of two and half times the amount. This is the 'tourism multiplier'.

3. Tourism Receipts and Balance of Payments

Most of the countries, specially the developing ones, have serious problems from time to time with the balance of their international payments. Much attention has come to be focussed on tourism because of its potentially important contribution to, and effect upon, the Balance of Payments. The basic source of information regarding receipts of a country from tourist arrivals and receipts is its balance of payment accounts. This information is shown in the travel account of the balance of payments statement, which shows the overall position of inflows and outflows and the final outcome arising from financial transactions of a country with the rest of the world. It is necessary to explain that in terms of balance of payments, receipts arising from expenditure of foreign tourists are equated with receipts arising from exports of merchandise (visible balance of trade), as well as other current transfers (invisible balance of trade). Thus exports of goods and services are comparable to exports of foreign tourism (or receipts therefrom) on account of foreign tourists visiting the host country and money spent by them during their stay, and imports of goods and services are comparable to imports of foreign tourism (or expenditure in other countries by the residents of a country going abroad). The travel account in the balance of payments statement incorporates:

(a) *The Credit Side*
This side showing the receipts arising from expenditure of tourists coming from other countries to the host country, and

(b) *The Debit Side*
The debit side showing the payments arising from expenditure incurred by the residents of the concerned country in other countries.

This travel account, however, indicates only how much foreign exchange was earned on travel account. It does not indicate the outflow (also known as 'leakage' in connection with the concept of Keynesian multiplier) of foreign exchange, on account of attempts made to attract the tourists and the connected expenditure. Table 1.2 shows the balance of payments on travel account and on the total current account for India from 1951-52 to 1981-82. The credit side of the travel account (or the receipts from foreign tourists in India) registered an advance from Rs 9.0 crores in 1951-52 to Rs 15.3 crores in 1960-61 and to Rs 94.0 crores in 1974-75. At present 1981-82 the amount was Rs 1063 crores.

4. Tourist Expenditure and GNP

Although the tourist promoting or servicing sectors have not been specifically given a place in the sector-wise statements of the Gross Domestic Product (GDP) of a country, there is a specific relationship between net foreign receipts from tourism (or income generated by the tourist servicing sectors) and the gross domestic product (income generated) of the country. This relationship can be illustrated by the following successive steps by which the expenditure incurred by the foreign tourist is converted into domestic income:

(i) Receipts of foreign exchange by the tourist servicing sectors which are equal to the value of final output sold to these tourists;

(ii) Expenditure or payments made on import content of the output, for meeting the import requirements of the

TABLE 1.2: India's Balance of Payments

(Rs in crores)

Year	*On Travel Account*			*On Total Current Account*			*Col. 2 as % of Col. 5*
	Credit	*Debit*	*Net balance*	*Credit*	*Debit*	*Net balance*	
1	*2*	*3*	*4*	*5*	*6*	*7*	*8*
1951-52	9.0	22.0	—13.0	908.9	1071.5	—162.6	0.99
1952-53	9.0	10.3	—01.3	795.3	735.1	+ 60.2	1.13
1953-54	7.3	13.4	—06.1	730.4	683.0	+ 47.4	1.00
1954-55	9.0	12.6	—03.6	795.2	789.2	+ 06.0	1.13
1955-56	11.8	12.1	—00.3	889.9	877.6	+ 12.3	1.13
1956-57	16.7	12.4	+04.3	898.6	1210.9	—312.3	1.86
1957-58	15.8	07.1	+08.7	992.4	1349.4	—427.0	1.59
1958-59	14.0	07.8	+06.2	827.4	1155.0	—327.6	1.69
1959-60	04.4	09.5	—05.1	870.2	1051.0	—180.8	0.51

(Contd.)

1	2	3	4	5	6	7	8
1960-61	15.3	12.1	+03.2	890.4	1282.8	—392.4	1.72
1961-62	15.0	11.4	+03.6	902.6	1209.0	—306.4	1.66
1962-63	15.6	11.7	+03.9	965.0	1319.0	—354.0	1.62
1963-64	16.7	10.6	+06.1	1127.5	1476.9	—349.4	1.48
1964-65	17.5	10.3	+07.2	1223.5	1675.5	—452.0	1.43
1965-66	15.1	10.8	+04.3	1129.3	1640.0	—510.7	1.34
1966-67	12.7	14.6	+01.9	1543.3	2389.2	—845.9	0.82
1967-78	20.1	15.0	+05.1	1690.4	2496.8	—806.4	1.19
1968-69	04.9	14.4	—09.5	1830.2	2195.4	—365.2	0.03
1969-70	31.7	15.2	+16.5	1841.4	2058.4	—217.0	1.72
1970-71	27.9	17.8	+10.1	1891.8	2223.2	—331.4	1.47
1971-72	31.5	19.5	+12.0	2095.8	2497.3	—401.5	1.50
1972-73	37.9	19.3	+18.6	2421.6	2673.2	—251.6	1.57
1973-74	56.5	17.0	+39.5	4607.2	3305.8	+1301.4	1.23
1974-75	94.0	15.1	+78.9	4078.8	4723.2	—644.4	2,30

1975-76	189.6	21.8	+167.8	5786.9	5492.7	+294.2	3.27
1976-77	285.0	38.2	+246.8	7287.1	5761.3	+1525.8	3.91
1977-78	530.0	44.4	+486.6	8240.2	6505.5	+1734.7	6.44
1978-79	564.8	64.7	+500.1	8702.5	8530.0	+172.5	6.49
1979-80	919.4	88.2	831.2	10755.3	10989.8	—234.5	8.54
1980-81	1165.6	90.3	1075.3	12466.6	14123.2	—1656.6	9.34
1981-82	1063.0	144.1	918.9	13577.5	15894.8	—2317.3	7.82

Source: Reserve Bank of India Bulletin, Bombay.

tourist servicing sector, excluding factor-payment abroad;

(iii) Gross Domestic Product (GDP) generated by the tourist servicing sectors, at market prices (i minus ii (a));

(iv) GDP generated by the tourist servicing sectors, at market prices (i minus ii (b));

(v) Indirect taxes less subsidies, including those paid/ received by the tourist servicing sectors;

(vi) GDP generated by the tourist servicing sectors at factor cost (iii minus v); and

(vii) GDP generated by the tourist servicing sectors at factor cost (iv minus v).

Items (iii) and (iv) constitute income generated or remaining in the country, which is equivalent to the net revenues in foreign exchange receipts from tourism without any deduction for the foreign exchange cost of investments. The gross product at factor cost generated at the tourist servicing sectors is distributed in the form of wages, and other labour charges, profits, rent and interest and provision for depreciation. Gross foreign exchange earnings from tourism, therefore, be expressed as a percentage of GDP or GNP.

5. **Foreign Exchange Earner**

Tourism is perhaps the only 'marketed' or 'marketable' transfer of funds, short of foreign grants, which can bring valuable foreign exchange to a country, without any exchange and export of merchandise. During the period 1951-81, India achieved a compound growth rate of 16.2 per cent in foreign exchange earning as against the world average of 13.5 per cent. In absolute terms, India's receipts increased from Rs 77 million to about Rs 7000 million in 1981. This may be a conservative estimate because RBI's latest estimate (for 1979-80) was over Rs 9000 million.[22]

Foreign exchange earning as a per cent of total invisible earnings of India is indicated in the Table 1.3.

The trend of growth in India in the last five years (1976-80) ending with 1980 is depicted in the Table 1.4.

Tourism also contributes to government revenues. There is

TABLE 1.3: **Foreign Exchange Earning**

Year	*Foreign Exchange Earnings (Rs in crores) Col. (i)*	*Invisible Export (Rs in crores) Col. (ii)*	*% of Col. (i) to Col. (ii) Col. (iii)*
1975	104.0	1609.5	06.4
1976	225.0	2154.0	10.4
1977	283.0	2806.0	10.1
1978	330.0	2938.9	11.2
1979	384 0	3071.1	12.5
1980	482.0	4420.0	10.9

Source: Department of Tourism, Ministry of Tourism & Civil Aviation, Government of India.
(The accounting year for foreign exchange earnings is Jan.-Dec., while it is April-March in the case of invisible export).

no official estimate of the figure, since most of the taxes are indirect. For example, every time a tourist goes sight-seeing or makes purchases, he is indirectly contributing to tax revenue by way of customs or excise duty and sales tax.

TOURISM AS AN INDUSTRY

G. Janata in a paper on tourism commented: "Tourism has arrived; aided and abetted by improved communications, education, higher incomes and freedom of movement, to influence . . . consumer behaviour and the growth, location, and stratification of the 'industry', including the hotel and catering industry."[23] This statement indicates the term 'industry' as applied to tourism. Strictly speaking, tourism, like recreation, is not an industry: it is an activity; but, in economic terms, it creates a demand or provides a market for a number of quite separate and varied industries. In some areas tourism represents the major part of the market, in others a complementary, but frequently highly profitable, demand for accommodation, catering, transport, entertainment, and

TABLE 1.4: **Vital Facts About Indian Tourism: Arrivals, Growth and Receipts**

Year	*Tourist Arrivals (Numbers)*	*Percentage of growth, over previous year*	*Tourists Arrivals in World ('000s)*	*Arrivals in India as % to World Arrivals*	*Gross Receipts from Tourism (In crores)*	*Percentage of growth over previous year*
1976	5,33,951	14.7	2,35,276	.23	225.0	—
1977	6,40,422	19.9	2,49,628	.26	283.0	25.8
1978	7,47,995	16.8	2,64,855	.28	330.0	16.6
1979	7,64,781	2.2	2,81,011	.27	384.0	16.3
1980	8,00,150	4.6	2,98,153	.27	482.0*	25.5
1981	8,53,148**	6.6	3,15,295E	.27		
1982	8,60,178**	0.8	3,32,438E	.25		

Source: Department of Tourism, Ministry of Tourism and Civil Aviation, Government of India, New Delhi.

* The figure of Rs 482 crores has been compiled by the Department of Tourism. This, however, doesn't include earnings from Pakistan and Bangla Desh also money spent by Indians domiciled abroad but still holding Indian Passport, and Foreign Airlines crews.

** Figures excludes nationals of Bangla Desh and Pakistan, including these, the total were 1,279,210 for 1981 and 1,288,162 for 1982.

E Estimated.

other services designed largely, perhaps even primarily, for a residential or industrial community. A model of the tourist industry is illustrated in Fig. 1.2.

If we look at tourism in terms of demand (or production) and supply, we can, say Janata, divide tourism into two sectors, the dynamic sector and the static sector.[24] Within the dynamic sector fall the economic activities of (i) the formation of the commodity; (ii) the motivation of demand; (iii) the provision of transport. Translated into practical terms, the dynamic aspects embrace the activities of tour operators, travel agents, transport undertakings and ancillary agencies. The static sector looks after the 'sojourn' part of tourism, the demand for accommodation, food and refreshment in the main, the chief provider of which is the hotel and catering industry, although there are also other ancillary services involved.

Many economic activities are involved in, and support, tourism, which for convenience we will now refer to as the tourist industry.

CHARACTER OF THE TOURIST INDUSTRY

First, tourism is 'a multi-dimensional phenomenon'; many and varied activities make their own separate and individual contribution to a comprehensive service to tourists. However, these activities, though separate, are interdependent. Such interdependence implies a need for co-operative effort and common policies, but "the diversity and . . . (small size) of many units make the formulation of any national plan by voluntary means impracticable and therefore uneconomic."[25] Nevertheless, some measure of co-operation and co-ordination has been achieved between tourist centres, hoteliers and tour operators.

Secondly, the industry is marked by a 'widely differing economic performance', tourism is dependent upon so many varied activities that a situation can arise "where weak links in the chain of services and facilities adversely affect the progress of otherwise healthy sectors of the industry."[26]

Thirdly, the industry is primarily a service industry and a large proportion of those actively engaged in it find employment in tertiary occupations, for example, catering, transport,

Fig. 1.2: A MODEL OF THE TOURIST INDUSTRY DEMAND

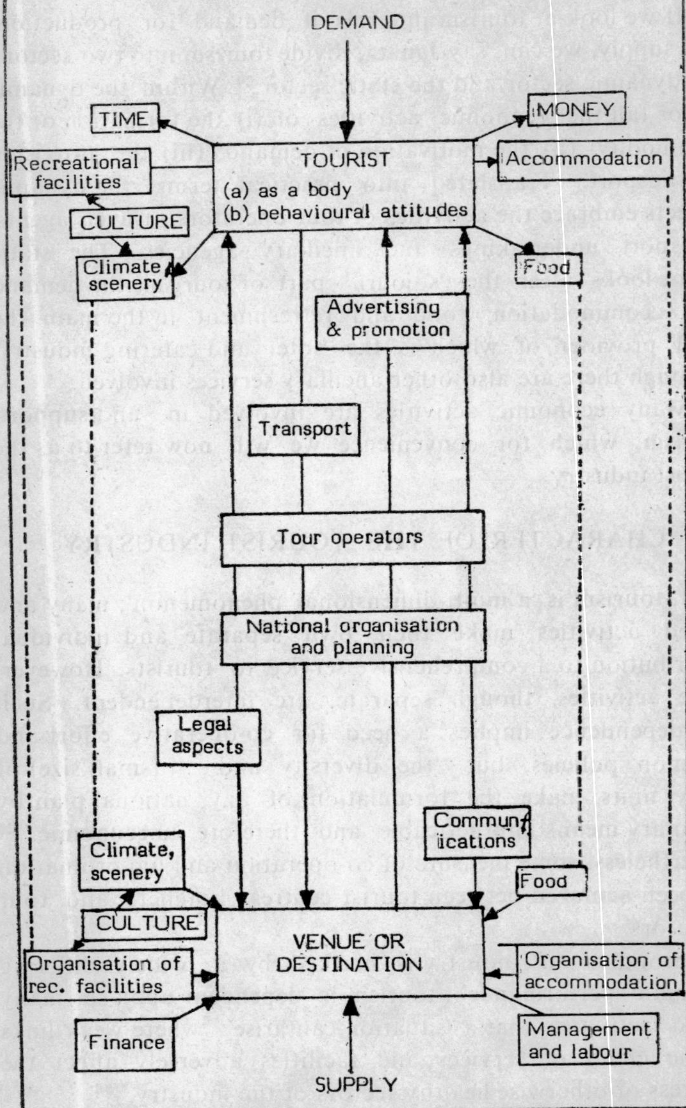

travel agency work. The industry is also marked by a fairly distinct seasonal rhythm: there are few places which have an all-year-round trade. This means that casual work and seasonal unemployment are often distinguishing features of the industry, especially in the typical resort town. This unsatisfactory situation could be improved by staggering of holidays, the promotion of second and out-of-season holidays at reduced prices, and such other measures. Anything which will help to lengthen the tourist season will help the industry generally.

Finally, the industry is essentially a dynamic one. It is dominated by the changing ideas and attitudes of its customers and must be prepared to show a much greater degree of sensitivity and willingness to adjust to new conditions than it has done in the past.

TOURISM IN INDIA

India has many attractions to offer to tourists of varying tastes and temperaments because of the unique and happy blending of the past and the present, places of extra-ordinary natural beauty, flora and fauna of all kinds, temples with delicate works of art, world-famous historical monuments and enchanting mausoleums like the Taj Mahal, ancient cities still retaining a great deal of their age-old splendour and mystique, colourful festivals—these and many other attractions are available for the tourists all across the length and breadth of the country. In India, tourism is considered the fifth largest export industry.

The balance of trade position of the country is fast deteriorating. Trade deficit during 1980-81, according to government estimates, was over Rs 5400 crores, primarily as a result of the sharp rise in the import bill on account of import of crude oil, fertilizers, cement, iron and steel, paper, aluminium, edible oils and such other items.[27]

Tourist traffic in India has been showing an encouraging trend ever since the 1950s when the foreign visitors numbered around one lakh. This was the first time when some serious efforts were made to make India known to people abroad. Soon after, however, it was realised that apart from catering to the requirements of the overseas tourists, steps had also to be taken to promote domestic tourism. The two go together in respect of infrastructural facilities. The Second Five Year Plan, therefore, accepted tourism as a national development endeavour. This led to the setting up of the India Tourism Development Corporation in 1966. The Table 1.5 provides facts about India's place in world tourism.

TABLE 1.5: **Tourist Traffic in India: 1951-1980**

Year	*Arrivals in India (Number)*	*Index*	*Arrivals in World ('000)*	*Arrivals in India as % to World Arrivals*
1951	16829	100	13185	0.13
955	33269	198	24010	0.14
960	123095	731	71139	0.17
1965	147900	879	115000	0.13
1970	280821	1669	169000	0.17
1975	465275	2765	221749	0.21
1980	800150	4755	298153	0.27

Source : Department of Tourism, Ministry of Tourism & Civil Aviation, Government of India.

The figures above vividly bring out the fact that though the tourist arrivals index in India has shown a phenomenal increase of about 47½ times as compared to the base year 1951, the country's share in terms of world arrivals presents a very low score of less than even 33 per cent.

The compound growth rate of tourist arrivals in India between 1951 and 1981 was 14 per cent as against the world average of 8.2 per cent, and India's share of world tourist traffic went up five-fold, but it is still a meagre 0.29 per cent. In absolute terms, India's foreign tourism went up from a 4.32 lakhs in 1961 to 1.28 million in 1981, inclusive of all tourists in the South Asia Region.[28]

NATIONAL DEVELOPMENT COUNCIL AND PLANNING

The National Development Council since its inception in 1952, has so far met several times. The Council has not made any direct reference to the subject of tourism in any of its meetings. Only indirect references to subject connected with tourism have been made in some of its meetings.

The establishment of the Planning Commission in the year 1950 and the introduction of planned methods for development of the country was an event of great significance. Although there was no provision for tourism during the First Five-Year Plan of 1951-56, the Second Five-Year Plan of 1956-61, provided an outlay of Rs 336.38 lakhs. The total outlay on Tourism, during the Third Five-Year Plan (1961-66) was Rs 800 lakhs. The allocation during the interregnum of 1966-69 was Rs 329.96 lakhs. Up to this period, the total outlays included both central as well as state sectors. However, the Tourism Plan formulated by the Department of Tourism for implementation during the subsequent Fourth and Fifth Plans included schemes that were taken up only in the central sector. The provision for tourist schemes in the sector was to be made separately in each State Plan. Owing to paucity of resources, the original outlay of Rs 40.35 crores during the Fourth Five-Year Plan (1969-74) was cut down to Rs 25 crores. The outlay for the Fifth Five-Year Plan (1974-79) was Rs 23.62 crores.

TOURISM UNDER VARIOUS FIVE YEAR PLANS

First Five-Year Plan (1951-56)

The First Five-Year Plan did not include any allocation for the development of tourism. The reasons for this are not difficult to understand. As tourism had not established itself as a separate entity, no need was felt to provide any outlay during the plan. During this period, the subject of tourism was looked after by the Ministry of Transport. The allocation made for transport included also the allocations for tourism. The Tourist Division which was founded in the year 1949 and placed under the Ministry of Transport had some provisions for expenditure on ways and means of attracting tourists from abroad. The measures adopted during the First Plan period to attract foreign tourists included bringing out a large variety of tourist publicity material, participation in exhibitions, screening of films, opening of tourist offices both in the country and overseas and involving travel agencies to organize tourist promotion activities.

Second Five-Year Plan (1956-61)

It is in this plan that funds were set aside separately for the development of tourism. Provision was made for the development of tourism both in central and state sectors. The main objectives of development of tourism during the Second Five-Year Plan were provision of accommodation and transport, and recreational facilities at important tourist centres, specially those situated in out-of-the-way places. These places were the sites of great monuments which were neither easily accessible nor were able to provide adequately comfortable means of accommodation.

Broadly, the tourist development schemes in the Second Five-Year Plan were categorised into three parts, viz. Part I, Part II and Part III schemes.

Part I schemes were intended to create facilities for foreign tourists, and were financed wholly by the Central Government. These schemes were centrally executed (directly by the centre) through the Central Public Works Department. However, in certain exceptional cases, the funds were placed at the disposal of the State Government and the schemes implemented through the State Public Works Department with 100 per cent grant from the Central Government.

Part II schemes were intended to create facilities for home tourists at centres which were also important from the point of view of foreign tourists. These schemes were jointly financed by the Centre and the State Government in the ratio of 50 : 50. The schemes were treated as centrally sponsored schemes, executed through the State Public Works Departments, and the Central Government subsidized the schemes to the extent of 50 per cent of the actual cost.

Part III schemes were included in the State Plans, and were wholly financed and executed by the State Government. These schemes were intended to provide facilities for home tourists at centres which were of local or regional importance such as Pilgrim centres and holiday camps.

The total outlay on tourism in the Second Five-Year Plan was Rs 336.38 lakhs, and the expenditure actually incurred was Rs 221.29 lakhs. The allocations and expenditure for Part I, II and III schemes are given in Table 1.6 and Table 1.7.[29]

TABLE 1.6: **Plan Allocation**

(Rs in lakhs)

Schemes	*Allocations*		
	Central sector	*State sector*	*Total*
Part I	83.50	—	83.50
Part II	74.44	74.44	148.88
Part III	—	104.00	104.00
Total	157.94	178.44	336.38

Source : Second Five-Year Plan, Planning Commission, Government of India, New Delhi, 1956.

TABLE 1.7: **Actual Expenditure Incurred**

(Rs in lakhs)

Schemes	*Expenditure*		
	Central sector	*State sector*	*Total*
Part I	37 46	—	37.46
Part II	49.42	49.41	98 83
Part III	—	85.00	85.00
Total	86.88	134.41	221.29

Source : Second Five-Year Plan, Planning Commission, Government of India, New Delhi, 1956.

Third Five-Year Plan (1961-66)

By the time the Third Five-Year Plan was launched in the year 1961, tourism had assumed increasing importance. The number of foreign tourists visiting India had considerably grown, and so had the foreign exchange earnings. The programmes of development of tourism included in the Secon Five-Year Plan aimed mainly at providing accommodatio transport and recreational facilities at important tourist centres. Provision was also made for the construction of road links to these centres.

The main objective of tourism development during the Third Five-Year Plan was provision of facilities for accommodation and transport. The schemes in the Central Sector provided for facilities at centres which were important from the point of view of foreign tourists, while those in the State Sector were intended mainly for home tourists. Provision was made for winter sports as Gulmarg in Jammu and Kashmir State. It was also felt that the expansion of the hotel industry had not been commensurate with the growing needs of tourism. During the Third Plan, measures were under consideration for assisting the industry with loans for construction of new hotels and for improvement or expansion of existing ones.

The total outlay on tourism in the Third Five-Year Plan was Rs 800 lakhs. Slightly less than one half of this amount was available for schemes to be taken up by the Central Department of Tourism and for grants to the State Governments. The remaining amount was to be spent as part of State Plans. Out of a total outlay of Rs 800 lakhs, the actual expenditure incurred was Rs 510.45 lakhs.[30]

The allocation and expenditure for Part I, II and III schemes are shown in Table 1.8 and Table 1.9.

TABLE 1.8: **Plan Allocation**

(*Rs in lakhs*)

Schemes	*Allocations*		
	Central sector	*State sector*	*Total*
Part I	292.00	—	292.00
Part II	58.00	58.00	116.00
Part III	—	392.00	392.00
Total	350.00	450.00	800.00

TABLE 1.9: **Actual Expenditure Incurred**

(*Rs in lakhs*)

Schemes	*Expenditure*		
	Central sector	*State sector*	*Total*
Part I	97.41	—	97.41
Part II	47.71	47.71	95.42
Part III	—	317.62	317.62
Total	145.12	365.33	510.45

Source : Third Five-Year Plan, Planning Commission, Government of India, New Delhi, 1966.

The Annual Plans (1966-69)

After the conclusion of the Third Five-Year Plan, three Annual Plans, 1966-67, 1967-68 and 1968-69 were launched. The allocation and expenditure during each of the three Annual Plans in respect of Part I, II and III schemes have been indicated in the Table 1.10, and Table 1.11.

TABLE 1.10: **Plan Allocation**

(*Rs in lakhs*)

Schemes/Year	*Allocation*		
	Central sector	*State sector*	*Total*
1	*2*	*3*	*4*
1966-67			
Part I	28.50	—	28.50
Part II	15.00	15.00	30.00
Part III*	—	—	—
Total	43.50	15.00	58.00
1967-68			
Part I	27.65	—	27.65
Part II	30.00	30.00	60.00
Part III*	—	—	—
Total	57.65	30 00	87.65

(*Contd.*)

1	2	3	4
1968-69			
Part I	111.31	—	111.31
Part II	36.25	36.25	72.50
Part III	—	—	—
Total	147.56	36.25	183.81

* Since Part III schemes were financed wholly by the State Governments, the Department of Tourism has no information on these schemes.

TABLE 1.11: **Actual Expenditure Incurred**

(*Rs in lakhs*)

Schemes/Year	*Expenditure*		
	Central sector	*State sector*	*Total*
1966-67			
Part I	8.69	—	8.69
Part II	9.86	9.86	19.72
Part III	—	—	—
Total	18.55	9.86	28.41
1967-68			
Part I	25.14	—	25.14
Part II	8.76	8.76	17.52
Part III	—	—	—
Total	33.90	8.76	42.66
1968-69			
Part I	35.42	—	35.42
Part II	15.82	15.82	31.64
Part III	—	—	—
Total	51.24	15.82	67.06

On careful examination, it can be seen that there is a big gap between outlay and expenditure figures. There was a heavy shortfall in expenditure not only during the Second and Third Plan periods, but during the three Annual Plans—both in the Central and State Sectors. Out of a total provision of Rs 336.38 lakhs and Rs 800 lakhs in both sectors during the second and the third plans, the extent of shortfall was of the order of Rs 115 lakhs and Rs 289.55 lakhs respectively, that is, about 34 per cent and 37.4 per cent during the two plan periods. The utilization of funds did not improve during the annual plan periods.

The shortfall in expenditure has been attributed to three main factors.

Firstly, the inadequate organizational set-up at the centre for the planning and implementation of tourist development schemes slowed down the execution of planned schemes.

Secondly, it was the declaration of emergency twice during the Third Plan period which resulted in tourist schemes being given very low priority both at the State and Centre levels. This caused delay in the execution of planned schemes. Some of the schemes had also to be dropped as a measure of economy.

Thirdly, delays often occurred in completing various formalities which precede actual execution of schemes.

These and some other factors were together responsible for the shortfall in expenditure during the Second and the Third Five-Year plans, and also the Annual Plans.

Fourth Plan (1969-74)

By the time of the launching of the Fourth Five-Year Plan in the year 1969, tourism had been recognised as an important means of earning foreign exchange. The broad approach to tourism in the Fourth Five-Year plan was to expand and improve tourist facilities in the country with a view to promoting 'destinational traffic' as distinct from 'transit traffic'. It was also proposed to take up integrated development of selected areas and encourage 'charter traffic'.

An outlay of Rs 25 crores was provided during the Fourth Five-Year Plan for central programmes. The programmes in the Central Plan included Rs 14 crores for programmes of the Central Department of Tourism and Rs 11 crores for the programmes of the India Tourism Development Corporation. For the states and Union territories, an outlay of Rs 11 crores was provided for during the Plan. The actual expenditure incurred was Rs 12.79 crores.

Fifth Five-Year Plan (1974-79)

The fact that tourism is the world's largest and most rapidly expanding industry was recognised at the time of launching the Fifth Five-Year Plan in the year 1974. It was also realised that the importance of tourism has been increasing mainly because of the growing affluence and leisure in the developed countries, and also due to the rapid development in transport facilities, and the declining trend in international airfares. The Fifth Five-Year Plan indicates the broad approach to planning of tourism which would generally hold good for subsequent plan periods. The investment priorities indicated in the Fifth Plan were :

1. Provision of additional accommodation and transport to match anticipated growth in international tourism;
2. The integrated development of selected new hill and beach resorts in order to accelerate the growth in the tourism and also to spread traffic over different regions of the country as far as possible; and
3. Tourism promotion abroad.

Keeping in view the guidelines indicated for tourism development in the Fifth Plan, the main emphasis in the Central Plan was on:

1. development of selected beach and mountain resorts such as Kovalam, Goa and Gulmarg;
2. development of selected archaeological centres of tourist importance;
3. facilities for tourists in wild-life sanctuaries;
4. loans to hotel projects and tourist transport operators in the private sectors; and
5. increased efforts in the direction of publicity and promotion abroad.

The major portion of allocation in the programme of the

I.T.D.C. is earmarked for providing more accommodation in the form of hotels, motels and travellers' lodges, in the state sector. The emphasis has to be on the development of places of local or regional importance.

The Planning Commission had proposed an outlay of Rs 133.24 crores for Tourism in the Central Sector in the Fifth Plan. This outlay was reduced to Rs 78 crores in the draft Fifth Plan, Rs 44 crores for the Department of Tourism and Rs 34 crores for the I.T.D.C. However, at the midterm review of the Fifth Plan in June 1976, the Tourism outlay was further reduced to Rs 40.74 crores, the share of the Central Department of Tourism being Rs 23.62 crores and that of I.T.D.C., Rs 17.12 crores. The utilization of funds by the Central Department of Tourism has been given in Table 1.12.

TABLE 1.12: **Utilization of Funds by the Central Department of Tourism**

(*Rs in Lakhs*)

Year	*Budget Estimate*	*Expenditure incurred*
1974-75	448.96	405.77
1975-76	418.75	336.52
1976-77	430.14	255.99
1977-78	499.00	480.00

Source : Fifth Five Year Plan, Planning Commission, Government of India, New Delhi.

It is clear from the table that during the year 1976-77, the utilization of funds by the Department was much less than in the previous years. This was, however, due to the need to exercise economy which resulted in a large surrender of funds earmarked for hotel loans. In physical terms, the achievements have been a substantial increase in accommodation and transport facilities to meet the requirements of international tourists. Fifteen Youth Hotels and Eleven Tourist Bunglows were constructed to cater to youth travel and middle-income-group tourists. Some of the other achievements included establishment of Gulmarg and Kovalam as resorts for increasing the volume of destination tourist traffic, development of facilities in five selected wildlife sanctuaries, development of the concept of environmental planning through the preparation of master-plans of twelve archaeological centres of tourist importance, opening of more tourist offices overseas for intensifying tourism promotion effort, and production of twenty-two million units of tourist literature for promotional purposes.

Draft Sixth Five-Year Plan (1978-83)—Revised

During the Sixth Five-Year Plan the objective is to consolidate the gains already achieved through vigorous promotion of India's tourist potential and to further develop tourist facilities.[31] The broad division of responsibilities between the Central and State Governments will continue to be the same as in the previous plans. The programmes intended primarily to stimulate international tourism will be in the Central Sector and those for the promotion of domestic tourism in both State and Central Sectors. Training facilities in various fields of tourism will be strengthened.

The annual growth rate of foreign tourism traffic in the next five years has been assumed at 15 per cent. On this basis, the tourist traffic is expected to increase from about 6.41 lakhs in 1977 to about 12.35 lakhs in 1982 and the requirement of additional hotel rooms has been estimated at 17,000. It is proposed to meet the additional demand of hotel rooms mainly through private sector investment. A provision of Rs 6.44 crores has been made for interest subsidy on loans to be advanced by the financial institutions to hoteliers for the construction of hotels.

In the Sixth Plan, the total provision for development of tourism is Rs 148 crores of which Rs 63 crores is for programmes for the Central Sector. Of this, Rs 30 crores is for the Department of Tourism and Rs 33 crores for the India Tourism Development Corporation (ITDC). The programmes of the Department of Tourism includes development of Dharmashallas, Youth Hostels, Sarais and some other items for the weaker sections of the population, cultural tourism such as Buddhist and other religious centres, wildlife tourism, Sports tourism, Social tourism, Promotion and Publicity abroad.

In the programme of the I.T.D.C., the major emphasis will be on consolidation of the existing hotels by undertaking suitable expansions, additions, alterations and improvements and taking steps to improve occupancy ratios. Provision has also been made for the construction of a Janata Hotel (Ashok Yatri Niwas) at New Delhi to provide low-cost accommodation to low budget tourists. Construction of new hotels, is being taken up only at selected places of tourist importance.

In the State Sector, an outlay of Rs 85 crores has been provided for promotion and development of domestic tourism. The programmes include construction of low-cost accommodation, provision of infrastructural facilities such as water and electric supply, new potential tourists' resorts to promote private investment, transportation for sightseeing, publicity and promotion. Facilities at places of Pilgrimage and on Yatra routes will receive special attention.

REFERENCES

1. S. Medlik, *Economic Importance of Tourism*, University of Surrey, Surrey, 1972, p. 18.
2. A.K. Bhatia, *Tourism in India—History and Development*, Sterling Publishers Pvt. Ltd., New Delhi, 1978, p. 130.
3. G.S. Singhania, 'The Role of Tourism in the Country's Development', *Indian Express* (Special Supplement on Travel, Trade and Tourism), New Delhi, 30 Sept. 1981.
4. R.W. McIntosh, '*Tourism: Principles, Practices, and Philosophies*, Grid, Inc. Colombus, Ohio, 1972, p. 182.
5. R.K. Chowdhary, 'Tourism Industry in India's Economic Development', *Foreign Trade Review*, Jan.-March 1973, p. 412.
6. R.C. Ummat, 'Fostering Tourism: Why Dither', *Eastern Economist*, Vol. 73, No. 16, 19 Oct. 1979, p. 804
7. G.H. Blake, & R.I. Lawless, 'Algerias Tourist Industry', *Geography*, Vol. 57, April 1972, pp. 148-52.
8. M. Peters, *International Tourism*, Hutchinson, London, 1969, p. 240.
9. H.G. Clements, *The Future of Tourism on the Pacific and the Far East*, Report Prepared by Checchi & Co., under contract with the United States Department of Commerce and Co-sponsored by the Pacific Area Travel Association, 1961.
10. *Economic Impact of Recreation, Vacation and Travel on New Hampshire*, Division of Economic Development, State of New Hampshire, 1962.

11. Paul G. Craig, The Future Growth of Hawaiian Tourism and Its Impact on the Neighbour Islands, Ph.D. Thesis, Economic Research Centre, University of Hawaii, 1963.
12. Daniel B. Suits, *An Econometric Model of the Greek Economy*, Centre of Economic Research, Athens, 1964.
13. *Master Plan for the Development of Tourism in Pakistan*, 1965.
14. *Study of the Economics of Tourism in Ireland*, 1966.
15. Pierre Gorra, *Nouvelle etude prospective sur l'apport due tourisme an developpement economique du Liban*, Department Researches et Documentation, O.N.T., Lebanon, 1967.
16. *Checchi & Company*, Washington D.C.
17. G. Richards, 'How Important is Tourism in Real Terms?', *Catering Times*, 3rd August, 1972.
18. NCAER, *Cost-Benefit Study of Tourism*, August 1975, p. 44.
19. M. Peters, *International Tourism*, Hutchinson, London, 1969, pp. 242-3.
20. H. Zinder, & associates, *The Future of Tourism in the Eastern Caribbean*, Washington U.S. Agency for International Development, May 1969.
21. S.P. Ahuja, & S.R. Saran, *Tourism in India—A Perspective to 1990*, The Institute of Economic & Market Research, New Delhi, December 1977, pp. 122-3.
22. K.K. Shrivastava, 'Tourism in India', *Yojana*, Vol. 27, No. 10, 1-15 June 1983, p. 7.
23. G. Janata, *Tourism in H.N.D. Hotel and Catering Administration Courses*, Paper read at Ealing Technical College, 1971.
24. Idem.
25. *Annual Report*, English Tourist Board, 1971, p. 18.
26. Idem.
27. G.H. Singhania, 'The Role of Tourism in Country's Development', *Indian Express* (Special Supplement on Travel, Trade and Tourism), New Delhi, 30 September 1981.
28. K.K. Shrivastava, 'Tourism in India', *Yojana*, Vol. 27, No. 10, 1-15 June 1983, p. 7.
29. *Second Five-Year Plan*, Planning Commission, Government of India, New Delhi, 1956, p. 480.
30. *Third Five-Year Plan*, Planning Commission, Government of India, New Delhi, 1961, pp. 565-6.
31. *Draft Sixth Five-Year Plan 1978-83* (Revised), Planning Commission, Government of India, New Delhi, 1979, pp. 400-1.

2

Review of Literature

Tourism is a manyfaceted phenomenon, involving many disciplines and multiple environments. It is for this reason that it throws challenges for its comprehensive coverage. Disciplinebased studies on tourism have been helpful academically and for specified area research. For a sound development of tourism it is necessary that the approach should be integrated. This would require the involvement of experts from various fields such as landscape-geographers, economists, sociologists, anthropologists, ecologists, environmentalists and flora-fauna experts.

There is no doubt that tourism has major effects on the economics of destination areas. Research focusses, primarily, on the economic aspect of the industry and this emphasis has resulted in a proportionately large number of studies of these effects. The majority of studies of economic impacts of tourism have been directed at international and national levels,[1] with fewer investigations at regional and local levels.[2] Although economic studies, such as Ogilvie's, were among the earliest reports on leisure and recreation, when compared with the latter, most economic studies are of comparatively recent origin.[3] In spite of recent increases, studies of tourism, particularly in North America, constitute only a small proportion of works on the broader topics on leisure and recreation. The early studies of Ogilvie,[4] Alexander[5] and Waugh[6] offered introductory statements on the economics of tourism but they did not provide a detailed examination of the full array of economic effects which have been available in recent publications.

G. Naqshband's article, 'Integration of Tourism and Environment', shows the relationship between the two. Of all the modern industries, tourism has the greatest need to protect the environment of the places of natural and cultural importance—be it a monument, a beach resort, or a wildlife sanctuary. The protection, development, and improvement of the various constituents of the environment of man are among the basic conditions for the development of tourism.[7]

R.C. Ummat in his article, 'Fostering Tourism; Why dither ?' surveys the growth of tourism in the country since the fifties when concerned efforts came to be made to foster it, and highlights those factors that have decelerated this growth. In view of the widening trade deficit, it is imperative that India should step up efforts at boosting the invisible foreign exchange earnings. Tourism, which yielded foreign exchange worth Rs 330 crores in 1978 offers greater scope for widening gap in the balance of payments. Unfortunately, it should in a decline in growth in 1979, to just 5.3 per cent from 16 per cent in 1978 and 20 per cent in 1977. The article also touches upon the economic benefits that can be derived from tourism, which undoubtedly can prove a good lever for enlarging the avenues of employment.[8]

The article entitled '3.5 Million Tourists ! Where Will They Stay ?' by T.C.A. Srinivasa Raghavan reveals the accommodation problem in the tourist industry, in India. The number of approved hotels in the country went up from 186 in 1963 to 354 in 1980. The room capacity increased from 7085 to 20860 between 1963 to 1980. But tourist arrivals in the country are much higher than the number of rooms available for them. The article also makes some suggestions for solving this problem.[9]

The article entitled, 'Promoting Tourism Through An Integrated Approach', by R.B.L. Garg reveals the approach by which tourism can be developed properly. Tourism development can become a positive factor for improving the economic condition and promoting development of a country. In many countries, especially in the developing countries, tourism has come to be recognized as an industry, providing employment opportunities and generating economic growth, besides earning foreign exchange. Therefore, in recent times, the governments have begun devoting attention to the promotion of tourism through an integrated approach.[10]

In another article, 'Bridging the Information Gap For Attracting Foreign Tourists', the author A.M. Roy comments on the existing system of information, which is very inefficient and defective, that a piece of information becomes almost outdated, when one approaches the country. Paradoxically, it is sometimes wrong. This upsets and annoys a tourist, who has ventured to travel and has spent his money and time. His experiences are different from what he had seen through published literature and information from travel agents and other government agencies.[11]

H.G. Clement, in his study, 'The Impact of Tourist Expenditure', says,

> In countries where there are substantial leakages for slow turnover, the money spent by tourists seems to turn over between 3.2 and 3.5 times a year before it disappears. In more highly developed economies, there is less leakage and a higher limit, perhaps 4.3 would probably apply. The multiplier of 3.2 is the lowest that can be produced under any reasonably accurate set of circumstances.[12]

John Bryden and Mike Faber during their study have observed,

> There is an evident confusion between the gross total arrived at by adding together the nominal value of a number of transactions (which economically, is an all-but-meaningless figure) and any addition to national income. The latter is arrived at by summing the value added in each of a sequence of economic processes. This confusion can only be described as a howler. It results in the double, treble or even multiple counting of benefits and largely contributes to the effect of 'multiplying the multiplier.'[13]

A tourism multiplier co-efficient of 3.2 for the State of Jammu and Kashmir, as assumed by National Council of Applied Economic Research in connection with its Techno Economic Survey of Jammu and Kashmir, may not be wide off the mark even considering that for Kashmir the 'leakages' may be slightly on the high side, because some of the goods and services on which the tourists spend have to be imported from outside the State, for example, foodgrains, butter, cheese, raw material for certain industrial products etc.[14] In fact, this can be broadly assume a marginal propensity to save of 0.12 for the State in accordance with the finds of the NCAER for the country as a whole and a marginal propensity to import of 0.16.[15]

The International Union of Official Travel Organizations (IUOTO) calculates in a study that the multiplier coefficient of tourist expenditure varies in different countries between 1.2 and 4.3.[16]

Similarly, the research term commissioned by the U.S. Government to study the effects of tourist expenditure in the Pacific area conducted a survey in seventeen countries in the Pacific Islands and the Far East. According to the survey, the initial spending, taking into consideration the re-spending by those who receive the 'tourist dollar's,' generated and sustained a level of economic activity, which was 3.2 to 4.4 times higher. The lower multiplier was valid for countries where there was a comparatively larger percentage of leakage of foreign exchange, and the higher multiplier applied to countries with little or no leakage.[17]

A paper by Andreas S. Gerakis, 'Effects of Exchange-Rate Devaluations and Revaluations on Receipts from Tourism', represents an attempt to evaluate the impact of changed relative prices of tourism services on the demand for international tourism. Gerakis observed that the impact of a change in relative prices of tourism services between rival tourist-receiving countries should be revealed by examining the pattern of receipts in the periods before and after a change in exchange rates. For each of the six countries chosen, Gerakis contrasted growth in receipts against those of the country's keenest rival and a group of close competitors. The approach adopted for the study has an advantage in that exchange rate changes should provide for the importance of wide movements in relative prices of tourism services.[18]

R.W. McIntosh, in his article, 'Some Tourism Economics' reveals the economic advantages from tourism. For the country, as a whole, tourism may prove to be a valuable source of foreign exchange; within a country, it may have a marked effect on the distribution of incomes between different regions, acting as an injection of spending power to under-developed areas. Employment opportunities may also be increased by tourism. Again, for underdeveloped parts of the country, the duration of employment through tourism may be a particularly important factor in the local labour market. Tourism may also support conservation. This will be mainly indirect; a proportion of the increased incomes of local inhabitants, business, firms and the local authority may be channelled through taxes into conservation work.[19]

H.P. Gray in his paper, 'The Balance of Payments Cost of Foreign Travel Expenditure', says,

> Assuming fixed rates of exchange and no induced price changes, the incremental purchase of a foreign goods or service will result in a net drain in the foreign currency reserve of the buying country. The proportional drain will result upon the marginal propensities of the selling nations to spend on domestic products, to import directly from the buying nation, to import from other nations, and upon the marginal propensities of these third nations to spend and to import and so on. The proportionate drain resulting from an increase in imports will be unity minus the ratio of incremental exports guaranteed per unit of imports. The rates of additional imports is called the reflection ratio. The reflection ratio can be expressed in terms of incremental imports from a single nation or of incremental imports of a single good or service; in the latter case the ratio is the average reflection ratio for all supplying nation weighted by the distribution of the incremental imports among those nations.[20]

P. Wilson in his survey report on, 'The Implications of

Tourism in India', discusses the economic, social and environmental implications of tourism in the context of the country. Tourism is an important economic activity earning very substantial and much needed foreign exchange for the country, besides providing considerable employment opportunities, and accelerating regional development. In addition, tourism is a dynamic factor of social progress and a great vehicle of knowledge and ideas, fostering goodwill among peoples around the world and within the country.[21]

R.W. Butler in his paper, 'The Social Implications of Tourism Development', discusses regarding one of the implications of tourism. Tourists generally come from more affluent communities. One of the social effects over a long period is that they influence the local population to adopt a way of life beyond their means. A process of acculturation starts between tourists and the indigenous societies.[22]

S. Medlik and V.T.C. Middleton in their article, 'The Tourist Product and Its Marketing Implications', discuss it in terms of the two factors of economics-demand and supply. The raw material necessary for the tourist product is completely different from that required by a normal industry and it is not possible to develop just any place, area or country in the field of tourism. International tourists coming from industrialised societies enjoying a much higher standard of living, have a different life style, and have much higher incomes. Their requirements are different from those of domestic tourists. Hence developing countries are compelled to provide two types of facilities: one for visitors coming from high per capita income countries with more or less equivalent standard of living, and the other for domestic tourists. The nature of the tourist product and its marketing implications, therefore, becomes complex. Even among foreign tourists, there is no uniformity of demand on facilities and services.[23]

D.S. Sharma in his article, 'How Banks Can Help Tourism', discusses their role and the way in which banks can help to promote tourism activity in the developing countries. Banks are associated with the business of tourism mainly through facilities to meet the financial needs of travellers. Expenditure on travel has, for a long period, been limited by exchange control regulations, the severity of which has varied from time to time. Foreign exchange may be made available in such forms as foreign currency, coins or travellers cheques throughout the world by banks. On the other side the government can also undertake to float tourist bonds and ensure the banks' participation in purchasing them. Subject to proper safeguards, banks can also be associated in the pre-investment activities in tourism development on a larger scale than at present.[24]

Prakash Narain, in his paper, 'Making Tourism More Profitable and Commercially Oriented', discusses how India should be able to earn additional foreign exchange, as well as provide employment through tourism. For this purpose, the Government has to increase the allocation, outlay in the Plan Periods annually. It is also necessary to improve the data base and the assessment machinery for making inter-sectoral comparisons and industry-wise analysis to make tourism and hotel organizations more profitable and commercially oriented.[25]

Ajit S. Gopal in his article, entitled, 'Indian Airlines and Tourism', discusses tourism in relation to the country's domestic airline, which is one of the vital links in the promotion of tourism. In the last decade the airline earned over Rs 200 crores in foreign exchange. In 1978-79 alone the figure crossed Rs 45 crores, forming over 30% of the total passenger revenue. Indian Airlines currently carries nearly 55 lakh passengers every year—approximately 17,000 passengers a day—a manifold increase in traffic since the mid 1960s, and this traffic is going up by about 24% every year.[26]

Another article entitled 'The Role of Travel Agents in the Promotion of Tourism', by S.S. Oberoi describes how the private sector is helpful in promoting and developing the tourist industry. The role of the travel agent is, primarily, to give advice to tourists on the merits of alternative destinations, on the modes of transport available and the routes to be followed for a given destination. He is also responsible for making necessary arrangements for a chosen/certain holiday, which may involve the booking of transport, accommodation, or other relevant services. Because the agent has accumulated knowledge, expertise and contacts, he is a useful and sometimes invaluable intermediary. The main role of the agent is as a retailer, that is, as a distributor of the tourism product;

while certain agents also act as 'manufacturers' of the products.[27]

J.N. Kohli in his article, 'Major Tourist' Attractions on South Eastern Railway' discusses the importance of South Eastern Railway Transport in promoting tourism. The Indian Railways are the largest rail network in Asia and the fourth largest in the world. In the country, the railways have been making continuous efforts for providing basic amenities for tourist rail-passengers. South Eastern Railway, with its sprawling network, has a fair share of the major tourist places in India. The Railway Ministry has taken steps to promote tourism in the South Eastern Zone (including the States—Andhra Pradesh, Karnataka, Tamilnadu, Orissa, Kerala, and some portions of Madhya Pradesh) by providing railway facilities to the nearest station of tourist centres.[28]

According to G.H. Blake and R.L. Lawless,

> One job will directly be created for every six new hotel beds, and many more indirectly. This is particularly important fact for some of less favoured parts of the country, notably the South, where employment opportunities are severally limited. Thus, tourism can be an essential feature of regional economic development at least in respect of creating work.[29]

F. Mitchell, in his paper, 'The Value of Tourism in East Africa' discusses the importance of tourism in three East African Countries—Uganda, Kenya and Tanzania. Each of these three countries has established a Tourist Development Organization to promote tourism through an integrated approach. The governments in these countries have encouraged private investment and provided public expenditure for the building of adequate accommodation facilities for tourists. The economy of each of these countries has not been affected directly by tourist industry as it is still in its initial stage as yet.[30]

It has been observed by W. Christaller, in his paper, 'Some Considerations—Tourist Location in Europe', that the development of tourism led to a large numbers of people being attracted to hill areas, which provided a new source of livelihood for the indigenous. This change came at a time when these hill regions were beginning to lose their populations because they were unable to compete with agricultural production in more favoured regions and farming provided a very precarious livelihood. Many other marginal areas have been likewise rescued from economic disaster and de-population through the development of tourism.[31]

A report, 'Tourism-Spain's Most Important Industry', by J. Naylon, describes the importance and significance of tourism for the Spanish economy. The foreign exchange earnings from tourism contribute about half of Spain's foreign currency account, and also help to correct adverse balance of payments and regional imbalances. The average rate of growth of the economy through the tourist industry in Spain during 1960-70 was about 6 per cent per annum. Without tourism, this might have been reduced to 3.8 per cent. Employment in hotels and restaurants was officially estimated at some 0.3 million, and in the field of indirect employment (shops, bars, etc.) the total might be as much as 0.5 million. Thus, tourism has proved to be a boon for Spanish economy.[32]

The article, 'Image As A Factor in Tourism Development', by John D. Hunt, discusses a research project which was designed to examine the phenomenon of 'image' as it may relate to tourism. It is a micro-study and is geographically specific in that it deals with the Rocky Mountain States and predominantly western recreational resources. The conclusion of the project/study shows that the fact and the perceived image of some state or tourist recreation region, characteristics may not necessarily be the same. Whether perceptions are right or wrong is not as important as what potential visitors believe and whether or not they are thought to be congenial to the recreation region. The uniqueness of an area is often considered a major asset in tourism development and promotion. While unique natural environments, human history, and culture often contribute to the success of a tourist recreation region, they could be overpowering to the point of distorting image and hindering successful development.[33]

S.N. Chib, in his article, 'Perspectives on Indian Tourism—I & II', discusses the character and the magnitude of the modern tourism phenomenon and the reason for taking an optimistic view of its future growth. Tourism is one of the fastest growing industries bringing in its fold many economic and non-economic benefits. India realised this truth very late when the race of development had run for quite some time. So that she may fill up the gap well in time, it is necessary to have a clear perspective.[34]

In a recent survey titled, 'Selling Benign Tourism: case References From Indian Scene', J.M. Ojha has described some important efforts that are being made for popularising foreign tourist traffic to India. The survey based on detailed interviews-cum-questionnaire method concerned itself with knowing: the causes of satisfaction and dissatisfaction, the pleasure and the problems which foreign tourists felt here. It was not so much aimed at checking reactions about infrastructural facilities as with various other factors which contributed to their psychological satisfaction or dissatisfaction.[35]

K.K. Shrivastava in his paper, 'Tourism in India', discusses the progress that tourism has made in India. The compound growth rate of tourist arrivals in India between 1951-81 was 14% as against the world average of 8.2%, and India's share of world tourist traffic went up five-fold, but, it is still a meagre 0.29%. During the same period, India achieved a compound growth rate of 16.2% in foreign exchange earning as against the world average of 13.5%.[36]

RESEARCH METHODOLOGY

The object of this study is to make an overall assessment of the economic (rather than the social, cultural, and psychological) impact of tourism, both domestic and foreign (but distinguishing between them) on a relatively backward region of the country, viz. the State of Madhya Pradesh. No reasonably comprehensive inquiry or study has yet been attempted in this sphere, and this survey/study may help in a realistic appraisal of the contribution made by the tourism sector to the economy of this industrially weak area, and thereby contribute to planning of tourism development programmes in the State.

DATA LIMITATIONS

The problems encountered in the study were numerous. These relate to conceptual difficulties, as well as difficulties of qualitative quantification and measurement, besides paucity of statistical information. For instance, a study of the pattern of home tourists in the State can be attempted only on the basis of currently available information regarding statistically recorded inflows. However, a part of the domestic traffic in the State, as elsewhere, is not registered, that is, those who stay with friends or relatives. Owing to this, the quantum of home tourists must be larger than that indicated by official data. Correspondingly there is an unrecorded tourist spending, the amount of which may be higher than the statistically registered traffic. Nonetheless, this spending must have some impact on the domestic economy but this is being totally missed.

A more important information-gap, in fact the most vital one, is the absence of data on tourist expenses (receipts from tourism in the State). The basic data limitation precludes one from an analysis of the importance of tourism in the State as a possible 'dynamic source' of foreign exchange, and a comparison of the growth rate of the aggregate income of the State and its income from the tourism sector in both real and nominal terms, i.e. a study of tourism's changing share in the State income. Accordingly, a satisfactory projection of the likely annual change in tourist receipts in the future becomes extremely difficult. Also, an inter-regional collation of proceeds from tourism is ruled out with this weak data base.

There are other crucial data limitations concerning State income, sectoral investments, taxes and employment relating to the tourism sector, which have materially affected the method of analysis. These have been brought out at appropriate places in the study. For instance, while some overall attempts have been made to evaluate the impact of tourism on employment formation in the State, it has not been possible to calculate the cost per job created in the sector as a whole, and the labour-intensity of that sector. For, besides elaborate employment figures, the investment and other expenditure per job created, are not available for the entire tourism sector in the State.

Also, a direct estimation of the impact of tourism on tax revenue has not been possible owing to the lack of detailed primary data necessary for the purpose and we have had to fall back upon the conventional procedure of relating tax revenue as a fixed ratio of the income originating from the economy of the State as a whole, and from the tourism sector.

METHODS OF DATA COLLECTION

However, to make the study meaningful, it is necessary to adopt suitable and proper methodology for collecting the relevant data. 'Indirect Oral Interviews' and 'Information from Correspondents'—methods have been used for intensive field survey, for getting correct statistical information, where it was not otherwise available.

Indirect Oral Interview method has been adopted mainly for the following reasons :

(a) absence of direct sources of information; and
(b) to ascertain the real position after taking into account the views of a number of persons concerned indirectly.

The other method of data collection, that is, Information from Correspondents', has been used as:

(a) this method is cheap and appropriate for extensive investigation; and
(b) relative information has to be obtained at regular intervals from the wide area concerned.

At places where information regarding the above two mentioned methods was not made available, for collecting the concerned relevant data, we had to make use of secondary information sources, provided by government and private agencies.

REFERENCES

1. (a) M. Peters, *International Tourism*, Hutchinson, London 1969.
   (b) H.P. Gray, *International Travel: International Trade*, Heath Lexington Books, Lexington, 1970.
   (c) H.L. Thuens, 'Notes on the Economics of International Tourism in Developing Countries', *Tourist Review*, 31 (3), 1976, pp. 2-10.
2. (a) B.H. Archer, S. Shea and R. Vane, *Tourism in Gwyneed: An Economic Study*, Institute of Economic Research, University College of Wales, Bangor, 1974.
   (b) D.M. Henderson, 'The Economic Impact of Tourism: A Case Study in Greater Toyside', *Research Report*, No. 13, Tourism and Recreation Research Unit, University of Edinburgh, 1975.
   (c) R. Vaughan, *The Economic Impact of Tourism in Edinburgh and Lothian Regions*, Scottish Tourist Board, Edinburgh, 1977.
   ——, *The Economic Impact of Edinburgh Festival—1976*, Scottish Tourist Board, Edinburgh, 1977.
3. F.W. Ogilvie, *The Tourist Movement—An Economic Study*, Stapless Press, London, 1933.
4. Idem.
5. L.M. Alexander, 'The Impact of Tourism on the Economy of Cape Cod, Massachusetts', *Economic Geography*, Vol. 29, 1953, pp. 320-26.
6. R.E. Waugh, *The American Traveller: More Darkness than Light*, Bureau of Business Research, University of Texas, Austin, 1962.
7. G. Naqshband, 'Integration of Tourism and Environment', *Eastern Economist*, Vol. 75, No. 24, 12 Dec. 1980, pp. 1297-1300.
8. R.C. Ummat, 'Fostering Tourism: Why dither', *Eastern Economist*, Vol. 73, No. 16, 19 October 1979, pp. 796-804.
9. T.C.A. Srinivasa Raghavan, '3.5 Million Tourist! Where Will They Stay?', *Eastern Economist*, Vol. 75, No. 24, 12 December 1980, pp. 1308-10.
10. R.B.L. Garg, Promoting Tourism Through An Integrated Approach, *Capital*, Vol. CLXXXI, No. 4523, 27 July 1978, pp. 1050-52.
11. A.M. Roy, Bridging the Information Gap for Attracting Foreign Tourists, *Capital*, Vol. CLXV, No. 4137, 5 November 1970, pp. 793-95.
12. H.G. Clement, The Impact of Tourist Expenditure, *Development Digest*, July 1971, pp. 71-81.
13. John Bryden, and Mike Faber, Multiplying the Tourist Multiplier, *Social and Economic Studies*, Vol. 20, No. 1, March 1971, pp. 61-82.

14. NCAER: *Techno-Economic Survey of Jammu and Kashmir*, New Delhi, 1969, p. 134.
15. NCAER: *Structure of Saving in India*, New Delhi, July 1973, p. 41.
16. *Economic Review of World Tourism*, IUOTO, 1968, Geneva, pp. 36-7.
17. *Report of the Ad-hoc Committee on Tourism*, New Delhi, 1963, p. 5, quoting the U.S. Department of Commerce publications: (i) The Anatomy of Tourism Today; (ii) The Future of Tourism in the Pacific and the Far East—*Reports prepared by the Pacific Area Travel Association*, U.S. Government, Washington D.C., 1961.
18. Andreas S. Gerakis, 'Effects of Exchange Rate Devaluation and Revaluations on Receipts from Tourism', *IMF Staff Papers*, XII, November 1965, pp. 365-84.
19. R.W. McIntosh, 'Some Tourism Economics', *The Cornell Quarterly*, Vol. 14, No. 2, August 1973, pp. 2-4.
20. H P. Gray, 'The Balance of Payments: Cost of Foreign Travel Expenditure', *Southern Economic Journal*, Vol. XXXIV, No. 1, July 1967, p. 17.
21. P. Wilson, 'Implications of Tourism in India', *Indian Journal of Marketing*, Vol. XI, No. 4, December 1980, pp. 7-10.
22. R.W. Butler, 'The Social Implications of Tourism Development', *Tourism Research*, Vol. 2, No. 2, 1974, pp. 48-61.
23. S. Medlik, and V.T.C. Middletone, 'The Tourist Product and Its Marketing Implications', *International Tourism Quarterly*, No. 3, 1973, pp. 28-35.
24. D.S. Sharma, 'How Banks Can Help Tourism', *The Banker*, Vol. XXVI, No. 6, August 1978, pp. 11-14.
25. Prakash Narain, 'Making Tourism More Profitable and Commercially Oriented', *Yojana*, Vol. 27, No. 9, 16-31 May 1983, pp. 11-12 & 29.
26. Ajit S. Gopal, 'Indian Airlines and Tourism', *Eastern Economist*, Vol. 73, No. 16, 19 October 1979, pp. 796-804.
27. S.S. Oberoi, 'The Role of Travel Agents in the Promotion of Tourism', *Capital*, Vol. CLXXXI, No. 4523, 27 July 1978, pp. 1052-54.
28. J.N. Kohli, 'Major Tourist Attractions in South Eastern Railways', *Capital*, Vol. CLXXXI, No. 4523, 27 July 1978, pp. 1048-49.
29. G.H. Blake, and R.L. Lawless, 'Algeria's Tourist Industry', *Geography*, Vol. 57, April 1972, pp. 148-52.
30. F. Mitchell, 'The Value of Tourism in East Africa', *East African Economic Review*, Vol. 2, No. 1, June 1970, pp. 1-21.
31. W. Christaller, 'Some Considerations of Tourist Location in Europe', *Regional Science Association*, Vol. XII, 1964, pp. 95-105.
32. J. Naylon, 'Tourism-Spain's Most Important Industry. *Geography*, Vol. 52, January 1967, pp. 23-40.
33. John D. Hunt, 'Image As A Factor in Tourism Development', *Tourism Recreation Research*, Vol. VII, No. 1, June 1982, pp. 1-6.

34. S.N. Chib, 'Perspectives on Indian Tourism—I', *Eastern Economist*, Vol. 77, No. 20, 13 November 1981, pp. 849-54.
——, 'Perspectives on Indian Tourism—II', *Eastern Economist*, Vol. 77, No. 20, 13 November 1981, pp. 903-09.
35. J.M. Ojha, 'Selling Beingn Tourism: Case References From Indian Scene', *Tourism Recreation Research*, Vol. VII, No. 1, June 1982, pp. 23-24.
36. K.K. Shrivastava, 'Tourism in India', *Yojana*, Vol. 27, No. 10, 1-15 June 1983, pp. 07-09.

3

Tourism in Madhya Pradesh

Madhya Pradesh as a State came into existence on 1st November 1956. The emergence of Madhya Pradesh as a State was an important event so far as the State economy is concerned because it comprises of 11 specific regions, namely: Bundelkhand; Bhaghelkhand; Chattisgarh; Malwa; Nimar; Mahakoshal; and 5 tribal areas, namely—Sarguja, Baster, Mandsaur, and Jhabua belt, Mandla and Seoni and the tribal area of Upper Shadol. These regions had their independent structured economy before the integration of the units. One thing which appears to be specific about these regions is that they have their independent cultures. Culture is a sum total of the natural surroundings, availability of means of subsistence, and the way of living. It is, therefore, a natural deduction that the region may possess potential enough to attract tourists. We find the following essential ingredients of the isolated specific attraction of the region concerned:

(i) Specific Topography;
(ii) Natural Condition;
(iii) Availability of Means of Communication;
(iv) Additional Feedback to Means of Survival;
(v) Artificial stimulation to Local Productivity;
(vi) Additional investment in the Local Market;
(vii) Additional Infrastructure Facilities;
(viii) Tourist-Based Industry;
(ix) Cultural Specificness;

(x) Information Centre;
(xi) Exchange between Specific Cultures;
(xii) Additional Economic Factors;
(xiii) Increase in Local Productivity; and
(xiv) Specific Independence of Tourist Economy.

To be specific, the State Economy of Madhya Pradesh in relation to tourism calls for attention to three significant factors to equilibrate the available forces between National and State economy:

(i) Tourist activity as fostering factor for the development of the State as well as National Economy;
(ii) Additional Marketing facilities in relation to tourism;
(iii) Marketable produce in relation to tourism.

Hence, the tourist industry, as a commercial factor, has its relevance to the economy of Madhya Pradesh.

RELEVANCE OF TOURISM IN THE REGIONAL ECONOMY OF MADHYA PRADESH

The term 'economy' is a comprehensive one, and includes several activities, processes, influences of interrelationship between means of subsistence available and their effective utilization for survival of man-as an individual and as a community. It can be regarded, in very simple terms, as the sum total of all those activities done by man with an intent to survive. The traditional concept of economics makes it a logic for justification of human activities for survival. These activities, according to the logic of economics, can be classified into three groups, viz.,

(i) Production activities;
(ii) Distributive activities; and
(iii) Consumption potential.

The economy of a country consists of two principal sectors—(i) Production potential and (ii) Distribution-cum-Consumption activities.

Modern economics is a combination of several activities that are designed for a continual survival of an organized group of human dwellings that can be briefly summarised as the sum total of the following activities:

(i) Local Production and Marketing, and
(ii) Local Consumption Areas and Productivity Parallels.

In other words, these can be termed 'Local Economic Activities'. This local economy comes under strain while it comes in interaction with other local economic forces. These economic forces necessarily travel through tourists—either domestic or foreign. Domestic tourists carry three of the economic forces with them, namely:

(i) Expansion of National Currency;
(ii) Cultural tradition; and
(iii) Exchange of ideas, and production relations.

While foreign tourists carry with them:

(i) Foreign Currency or foreign exchange;
(ii) Foreign Trade;
(iii) Expansion of International Economy or Exchange between National and International Economy; and
(iv) Apart from this, they carry with them certain cosmopolitan ethical principles which join the two different societies.

The variance in the tourist activity in a region or area naturally affects the organization of the State economy, and influences the monetary inflow in that part. Therefore, it appears proper to take into account the regional economy as the base for the construction of two model—A and B—in the microeconomy field to illustrate the relevance of tourism in the regional economy of Madhya Pradesh.

MODEL A

Part I State Economy as a Balancing Force of National and International Economy

In some conditions every area, where a place of tourist attraction is located, has its own economy besides the domestic area economy. These parallel economies affect the structure of the State Economy, that is, 'Organized efforts of a group of areas that comprise the State'. The State balances National Economy and International Economy on the one hand and Regional Purchasing Capacity (RPC) and Regional Marketing Facilities (RMF) on the other. This can very well be seen in Fig. 3.1.

The figure shows the impact of External Factors or 'E' on Feedback Agency or the control value, which is shown as 'a'. This 'a' is the sum total of the influx of money on a national scale, depicted as National Economy or 'A', and the interalia-exchange of national currency with foreign currency, shown as 'B'. This flow of currency or exchange is the result of Marketing Facilities or 'C', available in the region or area. The Regional Purchasing Capacity of inhabitants, shown as 'D' in the diagram, or Local Consumption Multiplier, necessarily affects the structure of monetary flow on the national economy, and

$\therefore$ A+D−B+C=Impact of E like tourism, on 'a'.

where A=National Economy;

B=International Economy;

C=Regional Marketing Facilities;

D=Regional Purchasing Facilities;

E=External Factors, and

a=State Economy or Feedback Agency.

The 'a', which has been designated as the State or Regional Economy, is the controlling factor of A and B in the sense that the flow of currency at the national level has its definite basis on the demand of the region. The commercial activities of a region naturally seek the excess flow of currency. This excess flow of currency in return increases the regional purchasing

Fig. 3.1: **MODEL A, PART I STATE ECONOMY AS A BALANCING FORCE OF NATIONAL AND INTERNATIONAL ECONOMY**

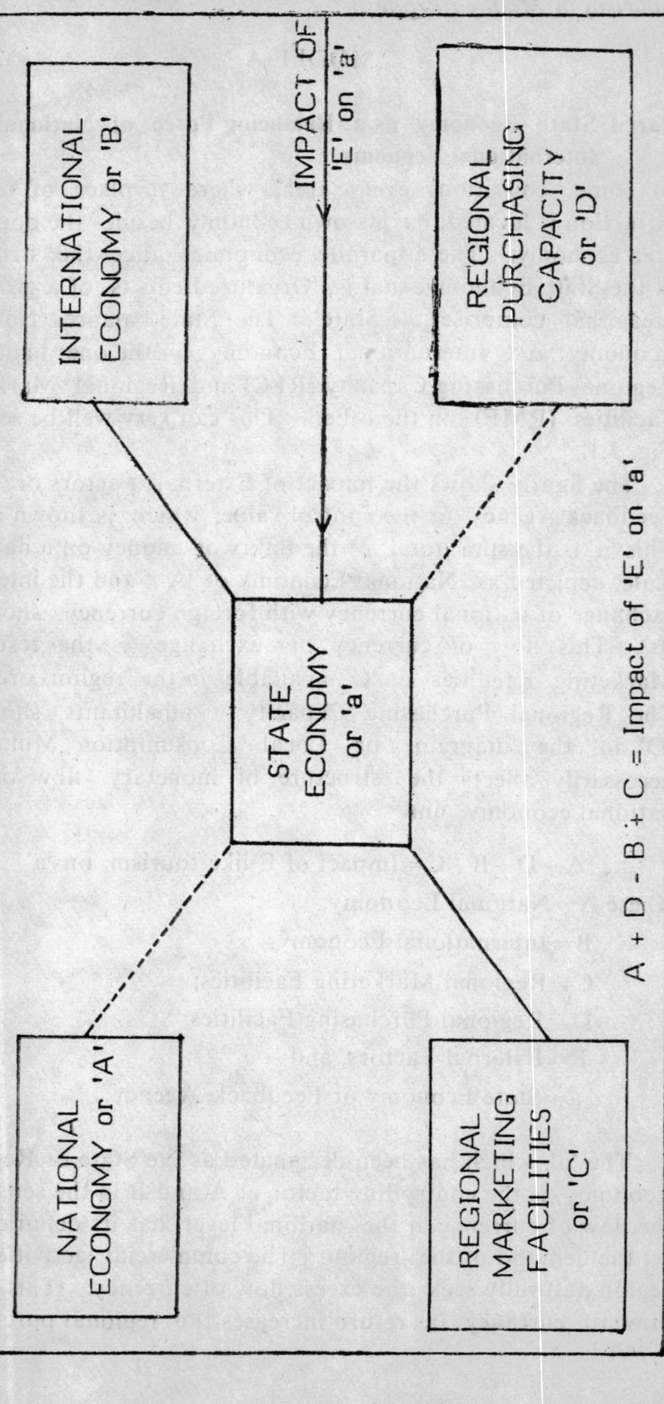

capacity. The local marketing facilities necessarily include foreign goods and services. This extra demand of foreign exchange is the net result of tourism and, therefore, it can be easily proved that 'a' is the net product of the excess flow of currency in the area, and increases regional purchasing capacity, deducting excess demand of foreign exchange which local marketing facilities require. The marketing activities in an area are the net result of the local feedback agency or local producing sectors. Therefore, the fact cannot be denied that 'a' is tremendously affected by 'E', if 'a' balances 'A', 'B' and 'D' with the help of 'C' which is the net result of 'E'.

Part II Area Economy

A State or Region comprises several areas that are connected with each other through transport and communication links. An area cannot have any transportation and communication links unless it has its Local Producing Sectors (LPSs). These local producing sectors serve as local feedback agencies for 'a'.

It is essential for the survival of local inhabitants that they should have local producing areas. Local producing areas necessarily imply adequate consumption and supply, and therefore, production and consumption go parallel.

LPS=CPP

where LPS=Local Producing Sector, and

CPP=Consumption & Production Parallel.

The forces of monetary flow necessarily include the Local Marketing Activities. The local marketing activities produce three kinds of effects : (i) Theoretical Background of Area Economy, i.e. Organized Area Economy on the basis of definite principles; (ii) With the help of Local Producing Sectors, the local market serves as a feedback agency of the State economy, and (iii) But marketing cannot foster itself unless it has adequate transportation and communication facilities and sufficient supply of goods, and therefore, the net result of LPS+LM=Supply, Consumption and extra facilities for tourists.

Fig. 3.2: **AREA ECONOMY: MODEL A, PART II**

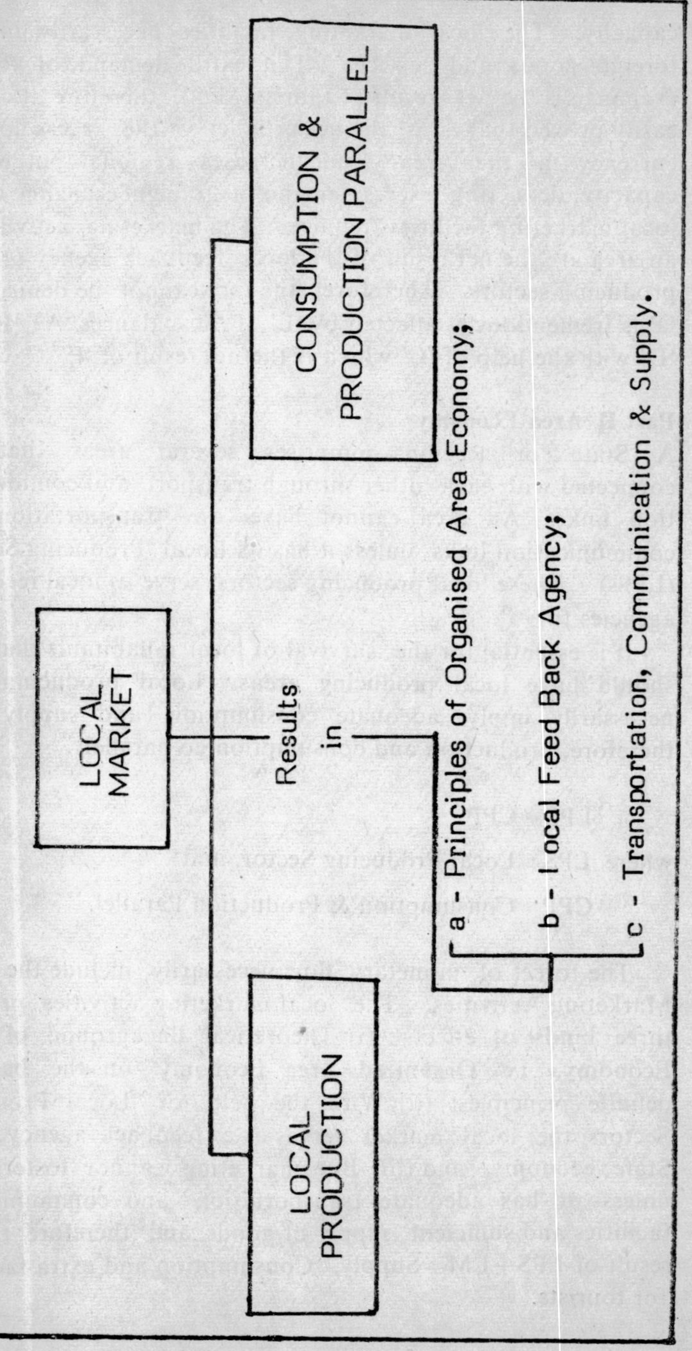

Part III Equilibrium of Consumption and Production as Affected by External Factors like Tourism

It is worthwhile to note that State or Regional Economy which comprises so many areas of area economy is greatly affected by external factors or 'E' like tourism, foreign exchange, foreign trade, and ethical factors like cultural exchange and cosmopolitan ethical principles. However, we are concerned with the economic effects of 'E', i.e. tourism, foreign exchange and foreign trade. Foreign trade has its own independent basis and it is not concerned with the present subject. Foreign exchange has its direct link with the tourist industry, and

$\therefore d_1 + d_3 - d_4 = d_2$

where d_1 = Topographical Features;

d_2 = Local Market;

d_3 = Communication Infrastructure and Transportation, and

d_4 = Local Accommodation Available.

$d_1 + d_3 - d_4 = d_2$ which is already affected by 'E', which builds up the structure of 'a'.

Part IV Increase in Local Consumption Multiplier due to Tourism

Part IV of Model A, reveals that external factor or 'E' affecting the Regional Economy, comprises of six major effects. These six factors are:

(a) Increase in Transportation Cost;
(b) Heavy Cost of Infrastructural Layout;
(c) Higher Pricing Level;
(d) Production of Luxury Items;
(e) Extra Marketing Facilities, and
(f) Excess Flow of Money.

(a) *Increase in Transportation Cost*

This is one of the essential factors that influence 'E' in the sense that, if the communication infrastructure in an area

Fig. 3.3: EQUILIBRIUM OF CONSUMPTION AND PRODUCTION AS AFFECTED BY EXTERNAL FACTORS LIKE TOURISM: MODEL A, PART III

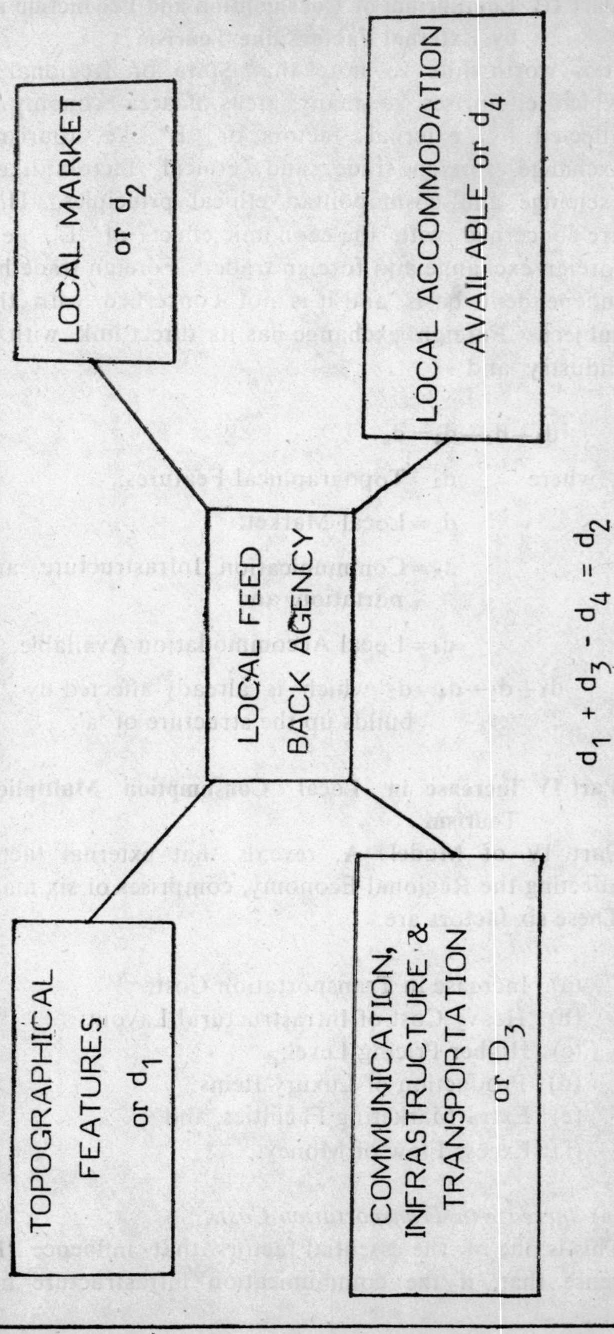

Fig. 3.4: INCREASE IN LOCAL CONSUMPTION MULTIPLIER DUE TO TOURISM; MODEL A, PART IV

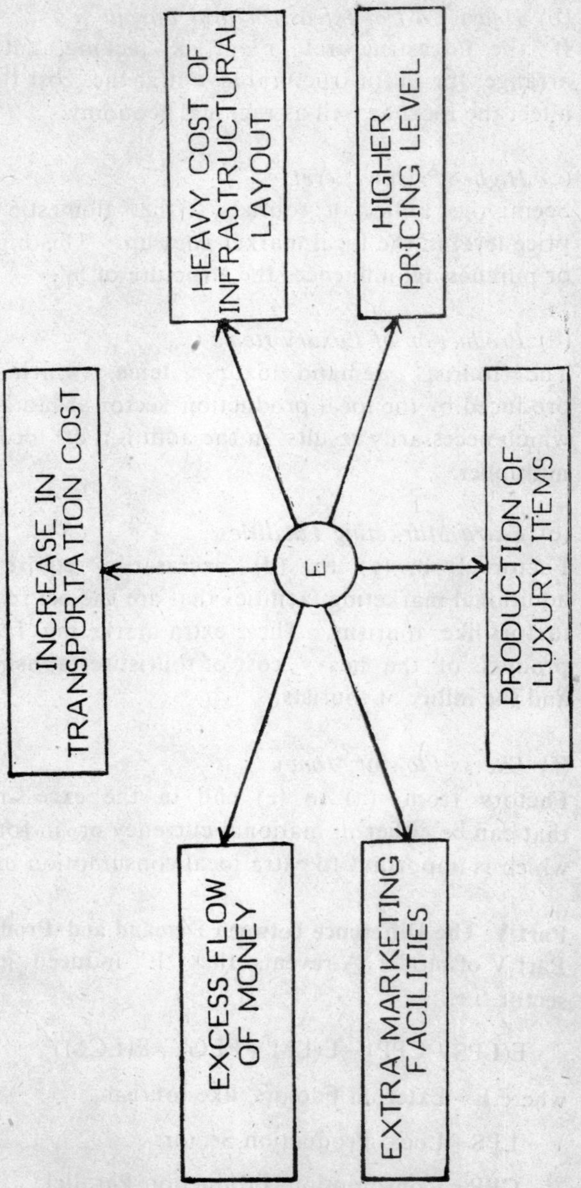

where tourist centre is located is not adequate, naturally the transportation cost would increase.

(b) *Heavy Cost of Infrastructural Layout*

If the infrastructural layout is lacking, naturally 'a' will arrange for infrastructural layout at the cost that can or may affect the local as well as regional economy.

(c) *Higher Pricing Level*

Seeing the influx of tourists, either domestic or foreign, the price level in the local market goes up. This higher price level or purchasing, influences the structure of 'a'.

(d) *Production of Luxury Items*

The tourists demand luxury items, which have to be produced by the local production sector at an additional cost, which necessarily results in the addition of local consumption multiplier.

(e) *Extra Marketing Facilities*

Factors from (a) to (d) necessarily require the extra or additional marketing facilities that are the net result of external factors like tourism. These extra marketing facilities are the products of the heavy cost of tourist establishment industry, and the influx of tourists.

(f) *Excess Flow of Money*

Factors from (a) to (e) end in the excess monetary flow that can be either in national currency or in foreign currency, which is important to extra local consumption multiplier.

Part V The Difference between Demand and Production

Part V of model A reveals that 'E' induced into Production sector, i.e.,

$$E(LPS+CPP)-E(LM+FEG)=E(LCM)^2,$$

where E=External Factors, like tourism;

LPS=Local Production Sector;

CPP=Consumption, Production Parallel;

LM = Local Market;
FEG = Foreign Exchange and Goods; and
LCM = Local Consumption Multiplier.

Fig. 3.5

MODEL A, PART V

THE DIFFERENCE BETWEEN DEMAND AND PRODUCTION

$$E(LPS + CPP) - E(LM + FEG) = E(LCM)^2$$

To illustrate the gap between production and marketing gives additional consumption multiplier which is the square of the domestic consumption multiplier.

Part VI The Square of Local Consumption Multiplier by the Effect of the Tourist Economy

This part of the Model elaborates two factors that are the basis of E(LCM). They are:

(i) $ELCME_1$, i.e. External Local Consumption Multiplier
(ii) $ELCMD_1$, i.e. Domestic Local Consumption Multiplier.

$ELCME_1$ reveals the structure of tourist economy, and in a symphonic manner $E \neq D$ ($ELCME_1$ is not equal to and is directly opposite to $ELCMD_1$ and therefore, the external factor cannot be equal to domestic factors).

$ELCMD_1$ consists of 2 factors:

(i) Increase in Local Consumption Multiplier or d_1
(ii) Excess Local Production Sectors based on tourism or d_2.

The ELCM of D_1 factor necessarily results in increase of ELCM, and therefore, the excess local production sector is the direct resultant of d_1 factor:

$\therefore ELCME_1 = ELCMD_1$ which is necessarily the resultant of te—$ELCME_1 = 2$ factors of $ELCMD_1$. The first factor that

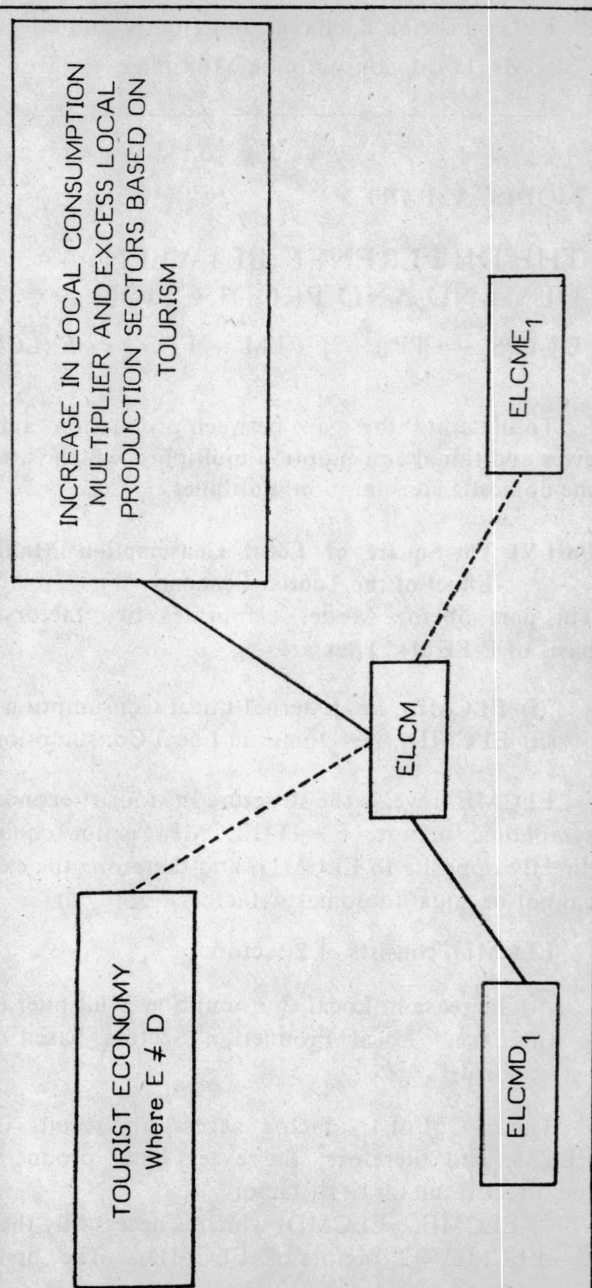

Fig. 3.6: THE SQUARE OF LOCAL CONSUMPTION MULTIPLIER WITH THE EFFECT OF THE TOURIST ECONOMY; MODEL A, PART VI

affects te—$ELCME_1$ is that of LCM affected by domestic consumption represented in D_1, hence, tourist economy (te) becomes the sum total of:

te—$ELCME_1$—increase in LPS based on 'E' which affects the D_1. It is possible only in the following two conditions:

(i) The domestic local consumption sector which works as domestic feedback agency and an extraordinary feedback known as external multiplier to ELCM. Hence $d_1+d_2=D_1$ and this D_1 is the resultant of the square of the external local consumption multiplier (ELCM) and gives tourist economy as a byproduct, where $E \neq D$.

(ii) When we compare $E \neq D$ and thereafter derive $E(LCM)^2$, we naturally reduce in a form where:

$$E \neq D_1$$

where d_1 and d_2 are the components of D_1

$$\therefore E \neq D_1.(d_1+d_2)$$

where E=External Factors, like tourism;

D_1=Domestic factors, comprises of d_1 & d_2

where d_1=Increase in Local Consumption Multiplier, and

d_2=Excess Local Production Sectors based on Tourism.

Part VII Tourist Economy in Relation to Total Economy

Part VII of Model A, illustrates two constant variants:

TE and te

where TE=Total Economy, and

te=Tourism as 'E' multiplier.

Total Economy or TE is the resultant of tourist economy as external factors plus domestic consumption multiplier, represented as 'D' multiplied by the sum total of two factors of 'D' known as d_1 and d_2, while the tourist economy with 'E' multiplier is the resultant of the derivation of the sum total of 'D' multiplied by d_1 and d_2 when subtracted from Total Economy.

Therefore, tourist economy is the direct resultant of Total Economy—Domestic Factors:

$\therefore$ te=TE−LCM. D (d_1+d_2)

where te=Tourist Economy with 'E' multiplier;

TE=Total Economy;

LCM=Local Consumption Multiplier;

D=Domestic Factors, comprises of d_1 and d_2

where d_1=Increase in Local Consumption Multiplier, and

d_2=Excess Local Production Sectors based on Tourism.

Fig. 3.7

MODEL A, PART VII

TOURIST ECONOMY IN RELATION TO TOTAL ECONOMY

$$TE = \dagger E + [\, D\, (\, d_1 + d_2\,)\,]$$

$$TE - [\, D\, (\, d_1 + d_2\,)\,] = \dagger E$$

$$\therefore \dagger E = TE - D\, (\, d_1 + d_2\,)$$

$$\therefore \dagger E = TE - LCM.\, D\, (\, d_1 + d_2\,)$$

MODEL B

The Model indicated in two parts describes the effect of tourism on the expansion of foreign exchange.

Part I Effect of External Factors on Total Economy with Special Reference to Foreign Exchange

As has been described earlier, the component factors of Total Economy (or TE) are three in number—Foreign Trade, Foreign Exchange and Tourism. If we take foreign exchange as a common factor for both, then tourism is not at all affected by foreign trade and, therefore, the external factor or 'E' is

Fig. 3.8

MODEL B, PART 1

EFFECT OF EXTERNAL FACTORS ON TOTAL ECONOMY WITH SPECIAL REFERENCE TO FOREIGN EXCHANGE

$$E = FT + (FE.\dagger)$$

$E - FT = FE.\dagger$ since $E - FT = E'$

$\therefore E' = FE.\dagger$ since $\dagger$ is a part of FE

$\therefore E' = \dagger$

---

the resultant of foreign trade plus foreign exchange multiplied by tourism or E=FT+FE.t. That is, total economy is the sum total of foreign trade and foreign exchange derived from tourism. Therefore, foreign trade subtracted from total economy gives tourist economy as a multiple of tourism. Since foreign exchange subtracted from total economy gives E′ which is a product of FE.tourist influx, E′ is the direct resultant of expansion of tourism resulting in expansion of foreign exchange. Hence, we can summarise Part I of Model B as E′=t.

Part II Foreign Exchange in Relation to Tourism

This part of the Model describes the interbalance of foreign exchange in relation to tourism, where it produces the following eight effects:

(i) Extension of Local Market;
(ii) Monetary Inter-exchange;
(iii) Bank and Foreign Exchange Control;
(iv) Tourist Facilities;
(v) Increase in Price Index—(a) in relation to Foreign Exchange (P_1) and (b) in relation to Local Consumption Multiplier (P_2);
(vi) Inflow of Number of Tourists;

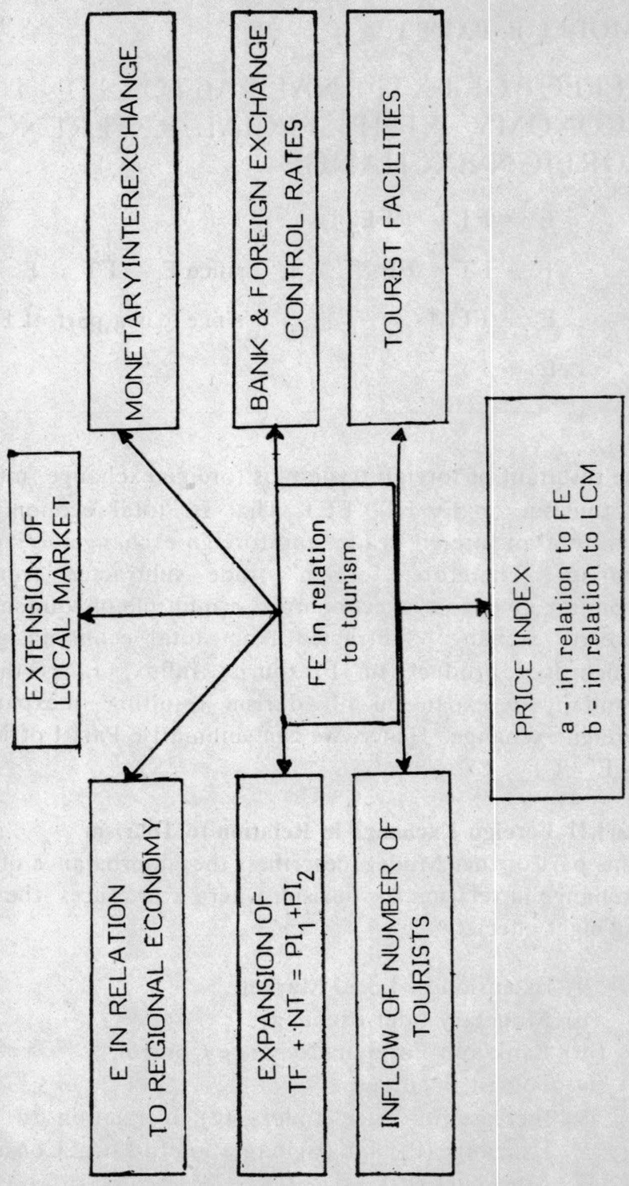

Fig. 3.9: FOREIGN EXCHANGE IN RELATION TO TOURISM; MODEL B, PART II

(vii) Expansion of Tourist Facilities plus Inflow of Number of Tourist which is equal to P_1+P_2, and

(viii) External Factor in relation to Regional Economy.

Therefore, it can easily be termed as:

$$TE=TF+NT-P_1+P_2=LCM.\ d_1+d_2.$$

where TE=Total Economy;

TF=Tourist Facilities;

NT=Inflow of Number of Tourists;

P_1=Price Index in relation to Foreign Exchange;

P_2=Price Index in relation to Local Consumption Multiplier;

LCM=Local Consumption Multiplier;

d_1=Domestic factor indicating increase in LCM;

d_2=Domestic factor indicating Excess Local Production Sectors based on Tourism.

The above formula indicates Total Economy or State Economy, which is directly the resultant of $TF+NT-P_1+P_2$ that derives LCM which works as a multiplier of d_1 and d_2.

CONCLUSIONS OF THE MODELS A AND B

The above models describe the functional economy in a Region or State, when it is affected by the external factors or 'E' like tourism. Both the models illustrate the role of tourism on every aspect of the economy. The monetary relations among the countries are the products of two factors:

(i) Domestic Consumption, and
(ii) External Influence.

Model A illustrates the effect of the external factors or 'E' like tourism, on regional economy. This model consists of 7 parts—each showing the extent of the role and importance of State economy in relation to tourism. The regional economy is the sum total of various areas like—non monetary economy; international exchange, regional marketing facilities and regional purchasing capacity. The regional economy is a byproduct of the interrelationship among the above mentioned 4 factors with adduced influence of 'E' and therefore, the necessary impact will be the emergence of the Local Market, as a balancing force between Local Production and the available gap between consumption and production parallel. In the construction of the regional economy and national economy infrastructure, the 'E' has its practical culmination in 6 factors that interbalance both theoretical and practical aspect of modern economics, and hence the logical conclusion can be stated as:

$$E\,(LPS+CPP)-E\,(LM+PEG)=E\,(LCM)^2$$

(the full meaning of these 6 abbreviations have been the same as given in Part V of Model A).

E (LCM) derives two basic factors known as $ELCME_1$ and $ELCMD_1$. $ELCME_1$ reveals the structure of tourist economy where external factors cannot be equal to domestic factors (or $E \neq D$). $ELCMD_1$ is composed of two factors d_1 and d_2, which generate additional flow of money in the domestic market due to external factors, like tourism. In this context, regional economy becomes the sum total of tourist economy plus domestic factors affecting local multiplier and, therefore, tourist economy is a derivation of the differentiating factors of total economy that is, domestic factors or $D_1 \, . \, (d_1+d_2)$ and external factors or 'E' like tourism.

Model B takes one of the factors of tourist economy as its base, and this factor is foreign exchange, in relation to tourism. In its applicability, the 'E' is the culmination of $FT+(FE\,.\,t)$, and this portion of the model concludes with the result $E'=t$ (in which E' is the sum total of $E-Ft$ and t is a part of foreign exchange). The second part of this model reveals the impact of factor t, known as tourism, on foreign exchange which in return gives 8 effects. These 8 effects mainly comprise additional influx in local market, based on monetary inflow due to increase in the number of tourists, with a natural result of increase in price levels, which adduces additional importance to LCM in relation to d_1 and d_2.

The above models when reduced to the logical conclusion reveal that this organized sector of tourism in various plan periods in the State of Madhya Pradesh has not been allocated enough monetary provision as required, in spite of the fact that tourism has an important role for the development of the regional as well as area economy of Madhya Pradesh.

DEVELOPMENT AND PROGRESS OF TOURISM DURING THE STATE FIVE-YEAR PLAN PERIODS

The development of tourism in the State was started at the beginning of the *Third Five-Year Plan* (*1961-66*) as the Directorate of Tourism came into existence in 1961. The total provision under this head for the Third Plan Period was Rs 22.97 lakhs. This total provision was divided into three part schemes: Rs 9.25 lakhs were allocated for part I schemes (to be fully financed by the Government of India); Rs 3.72 lakhs for part II schemes (50% cost-sharing basis between the Centre and the State), and Rs 10 lakhs for part III schemes (fully financed by the State Government). The Government of India, during the midterm plan, decided to abandon schemes and, hence, no expenditure was incurred on the outlay provided for part I schemes. Out of the total provision of 13.97 lakhs in part II and III schemes, an expenditure of Rs 4.59 lakhs was incurred for construction of Tourist Bungalows at Khajuraho, Mandu, and Chitrakoot, purchase of vehicles for transport and establishment of Tourist Offices at Bhopal, Gwalior and Indore.

Table 3.1 shows the plan allocation, the budget provision and the actual expenditure incurred during the Third Plan Period on tourism.

ANNUAL PLANS (1966-69)

During the Annual Plans, a total provision of Rs 14.34 lakhs was sanctioned, out of which Rs 10.24 lakhs were spent. This expenditure was incurred on construction and improvement of internal roads, construction of 45 Holiday Homes at Pachmarhi;

TABLE 3.1

(*Rs in Lakhs*)

Year	*Plan Allocation*	*Budget Provision*	*Actual Expenditure*
1961-62	1.27	1.41	0.68
1962-63	1.50	1.21	1.00
1963-64	1.25	1.15	0.67
1964-65	5.99	5.29	1.15
1965-66	2.00	1.80	1.08
Total	12.01	10.86	4.58

Source: Directorate of Tourism, Madhya Pradesh, Bhopal.

a Rest House at Kanha; boating facilities at Bhopal; transport and publication of transparency sets for Sanchi and Mandu.

The following Table 3.2 shows the outlay and the expenditure on tourism during the Annual Plans:

TABLE 3.2

(*Rs in Lakhs*)

Year	*Plan Allocation*	*Budget Provision*	*Actual Expenditure*
1966-67	4.50	4.50	3.93
1967-68	4.62	4.62	2.49
1968-69	5.22	5.22	3.82
Total	14.34	14.34	10.24

Source: Directorate of Tourism, Madhya Pradesh, Bhopal.

FOURTH FIVE-YEAR PLAN (1969-74)

In the Fourth Plan Period, the State Government had allocated a total outlay of Rs 70 lakhs for the development of tourism.

An expenditure of Rs 48.39 lakhs was incurred on the following tourist places:

(i) Khajuraho: construction of dormitory; improvement of Premsagar and Shivsagar tanks; land acquisition and construction of bypass road.

(ii) Kanha: construction of Youth Hostel and Tourist Cottages; improvement of Forest Rest House, construction of roads, petrol pump, and veterinary hospital.

(iii) Bhopal: construction of Boat House and purchase of some new boats.

(iv) Pachmarhi, Damoh, Sanchi, Gwalior, Mandu and Onkareshwar were the other places of tourist interest on which the State Government had spent money to make them upto date and to provide necessary facilities for attracting more tourists.

(v) Transport: Operation of cars, and tourist coaches and purchase of some new vehicles.

(vi) Publicity: Advertisements, and publication of folders and picture post-cards.

Besides these, during the Plan Period efforts have been made to provide some necessary facilities for the religious centres.

Table 3.3 indicates the plan, budget and actual expenditure picture for the promotion of tourism in the State.

TABLE 3.3

(*Rs in Lakhs*)

Year	*Plan Allocation*	*Budget Provision*	*Actual Expenditure*
1969-70	3.46	3.45	2.70
1970-71	5.76	6.38	4.69
1971-72	21.54	21.74	11.37
1972-73	24.30	24.30	17.56
1973-74	26.45	26.45	12.07
Total	81.51	82.32	48.39

Source: Directorate of Tourism, Madhya Pradesh, Bhopal.

FIFTH FIVE-YEAR PLAN (1974-79)

The Fifth Five-Year Plan brought alongwith it a bigger outlay of Rs 140.00 lakhs. This outlay was exceeded by the total of the annual plan allocations given, during the Five Years, and hence the expenditure incurred was Rs 150.38 lakhs. The following schemes were taken up by the Government:

(i) Formation and establishment of the Madhya Pradesh State Tourism Development Corporation with sanction of the first instalment of share capital contribution;
(ii) In the ten tourist places—Khajuraho, Mandu, Kanha, Gwalior, Bhedaghat, Pachmarhi, Bhoramdeo, Bandhavgarh, Chitrakoot, and Mandu—the Government had decided to provide modern facilities to attract more foreign and domestic tourists; and
(iii) Construction of Motels at Ujjain, Raipur, Shivpuri, Kanha, Bhedaghat, Bandhavgarh, Satna, Pachmarhi, Sagar and Jagdalpur.

The Table 3.4 shows the annual outlay and actual expenditure incurred during the Fifth Five-Year Plan.

TABLE 3.4

(Rs in Lakhs)

Year	*Plan Allocation*	*Budget Provision*	*Actual Expenditure*
1974-75	11.00	11.00	6.05
1975-76	10.00	10.00	10.22
1976-77	16.00	29.50	24.40
1977-78	55.00	55.00	54.70
1978-79	56.40	56.40	55.01
Total	148.40	161.90	150.38

Source: Directorate of Tourism, Madhya Pradesh, Bhopal.

During this plan period, the concentration was on developing the infrastructure and facilities at the tourist places. It was found that a few major tourist centres still did not have basic amenities such as electricity, water, approach roads. These were provided at places like Khajuraho, Kanha, Pachmarhi, Mandu and Bhormadeo. Facilities in the form of tourist bungalows and log-huts were constructed at Khajuraho, Kanha, Gwalior and Pachmarhi. The State Government, increasingly aware of the economic importance of tourism, decided to set up the Tourism Development Corporation, so that additional funds for investment could be obtained through institutional finance.

ANNUAL PLAN (1979-80)

In the year 1979-80, a sum of Rs 80 lakhs was allocated. The new feature were: share capital contribution to the Madhya Pradesh State Tourism Development Corporation (Rs 43 lakhs); loan to the Corporation for tribal sub-plan schemes (Rs 3 lakhs); floodlighting and provision of approach road to Bhedaghat (Rs 2.50 lakhs); development of regional and local centres (Rs 2.00 lakhs), and approach road to Khajuraho (Rs 1.48 lakhs). The residual amount of Rs 24.02 lakhs was for the completion of the continuing schemes and for grant-in-aid to the corporation for the operation of tourist accommodation. The new schemes were implemented and the continuing schemes were completed during the year at a total expenditure of Rs 77.82 lakhs.

The Table 3.5 shows the outlay and the expenditure incurred during this annual plan period.

TABLE 3.5

(*Rs in Lakhs*)

Year	*Plan Allocation*	*Budget Provision*	*Actual Expenditure*
1979-80	80.00	80 00	77.57
Total	80.00	80.00	77.57

Source: Directorate of Tourism. Madhya Pradesh, Bhopal.

SIXTH FIVE-YEAR PLAN (1980-85)

In the Sixth Plan, the tourism sector has been allocated Rs 588.84 lakhs. The main objective of this plan is to provide the necessary basic facilities to develop the infrastructure to attract more foreign as well as domestic tourists. The growth rate has been fixed around 10% per annum. Basic transport facilities like road construction, railway stations joining the important places have been given much importance during the plan period. As far as Civil Aviation is concerned, Khajuraho is served by a daily Boeing Flight and Jabalpur, Raipur, Indore and Bhopal through Avro Services from Delhi, Bombay, Calcutta and Madras.

The variety of attractions and the size of the State require a selective approach in planning for the development of tourism infrastructure. It is, therefore, proposed that some places with outstanding attraction would be given priority in development. Tourist places like Khajuraho, Kanha, Sanchi-Bhopal, Mandu-Indore, Gwalior-Shivpuri, Pachmarhi, and Bandhavgarh have been included in this category. The second phase would pay attention for the remaining places—Amarkantak, Ujjain, Onkareshwar-Maheshwar, Chitrakoot, Bhedaghat, Jagdalpur, Chitrakoot, and Orchha.

The Table 3.6 shows the plan allocation, the budget provision and actual expenditure incurred during the Sixth Five-Year Plan.

TABLE 3.6

(*Rs. in Lakhs*)

Year	*Plan Allocation*	*Budget Provision*	*Actual Expenditure*
1980-81	85.00	85.00	83.70
1981-82	100.00	100.00	102.35
1982-83	120.00	146.61	145.22
1983-84	135.00	135.00	132.16
1984-85	180.00*	180.00*	—

*Provisional.

Source: Directorate of Tourism, Madhya Pradesh, Bhopal.

During the first annual plan year of the Sixth Plan Period, 1980-81, an expenditure of Rs 83.70 lakhs was incurred against an outlay of Rs 85.00 lakhs. Out of this allotment, the Tourism Development Corporation was given the share capital contribution for additional accommodation, improvement of existing accommodation and the provision of transport facilities at selected tourist centres. Grant-in-aid was also given to the Corporation for publicity, entertainment and operation of tourist accommodation. The local bodies at the tourist centres of Orchha, Maheshwar, Pachmarhi, Bhedaghat, Khajuraho, Rahatgarh and Mandu were provided funds for the creation of basic tourist amenities. Water supply facilities were provided at Kanha, and Bandhavagarh National Parks, and the first phase of infrastructural facilities was provided for the centrally-sponsored scheme of a forest-lodge at Kanha.

In the second annual plan year of the Sixth Plan Period, 1981-82; the outlay and budget provision was Rs. 100 lakhs for the following schemes:

(*Rs in Lakhs*)

S. No.	*Name of Scheme*	*Outlay*
1.	Share Capital Contribution to the M.P.T.D.C.	56.39
2.	Grant-in-aid to the Corporation for:	
	(a) Publicity and Promotion	06.00
	(b) Operation of tourist accommodation	01.50
	(c) Tourist entertainment	01.50
3.	Grant-in-aid to the local bodies for development of basic amenities	08.35
4.	Floodlighting at Marble Rocks	03.00
5.	State Share for Tourist Village at Shivpuri	01.00
6.	Operation of Youth Hostels	00.60
	Total	Rs 78.34

(*Contd.*)

S. No.	*Name of Scheme*	*Outlay*
Tribal Sub Plan:		
1.	Share Capital Contribution to the Corporation	18.61
2.	State Share for the Forest Lodge at Mukki	02.00
3.	Minor Original Works	00.50
4.	Water Supply at Kanha	00.50
5.	Handicraft items for Kanha	00.05
	Total	Rs 21.66

Source: Directorate of Tourism, Madhya Pradesh, Bhopal.

It is anticipated that the provision would be fully utilized by the end of the financial year. Plan allocation, budget provision and actual expenditure incurred during the different State Plan Periods is shown in the graph.

TOURISM DEVELOPMENT CORPORATION

Madhya Pradesh State Tourism Development Corporation Limited, was set up in 1978 so that the share capital contributions received from the Government should be supplemented by institutional finance for the development schemes and a measure of flexibility is introduced in the management of tourists facilities. This would result in the speedy expansion of the facilities and systematic management of facilities to cater to the need of tourists. In the State like Madhya Pradesh, which has the problems of size, poor communication and merger tourist facilities, the Corporation will have to play a vital role in the promotion and development of tourist places. Hence, it should not be solely viewed from the angle of a profitable commercial undertaking.

The Corporation is presently engaged in the management of existing tourist accommodation, operation of tourist transport facilities, development of additional tourist facilities and wider promotion of tourist attractions through advertisements, publication of tourists literature and tourist information

Fig. 3.10: PLAN ALLOCATION, BUDGET PROVISION AND ACTUAL EXPENDITURE DURING THE STATE PLAN PERIODS

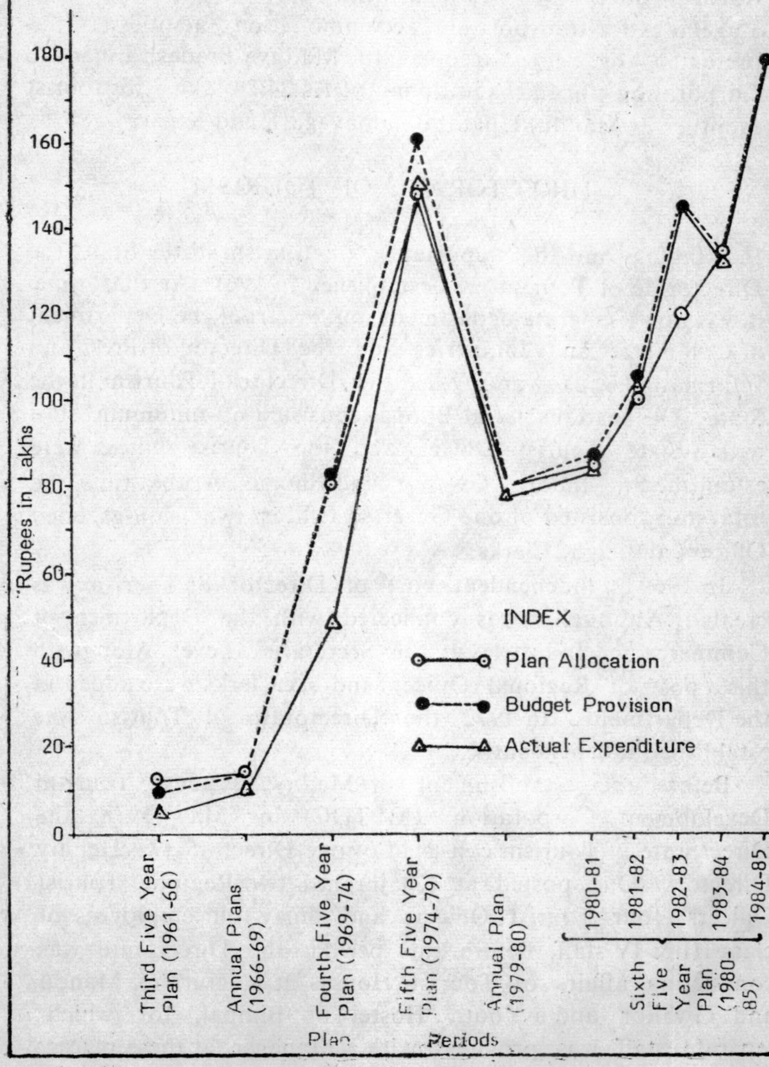

offices. The State Government has so far given Rs 145.15 lakhs as share capital contribution, Rs 38.80 lakhs as grant for publicity, Rs 38.16 lakhs as grant for operation of tourist accommodation and entertainment and transport and Rs 20.16 lakhs as loans.

The Corporation has obtained Rs 15.92 lakhs as institutional finance from Madhya Pradesh Financial Corporation and Banks for transport and accommodation facilities. It has presented the project reports to Madhya Pradesh Financial Corporation for an additional of Rs 24.24 lakhs for tourist facilities at Mandu, Ujjain, Bandhavagarh and Sagar.

DIRECTORATE OF TOURISM

In bringing out the importance of tourism in the State, the Directorate of Tourism was established in 1961. At that time, it was not a separate department, but a part of the Department of Commerce and Industries and the Director of Press and Information was working as the Director of Tourism in the State. The headquarter at Bhopal consisted of minimum staff with a State Tourist Officer and the Tourist Offices were established in Indore, Gwalior and Bhopal. At that time, the total staff consisted of one Gazetted Officer, two Non-gazetted Officers and eight Clerks.

In 1969 an independent post of Director of Tourism was created. Although it was connected with the Department of Commerce and Industries at the Secretariat Level. Alongwith this a post of Regional Officer and six Clerks were added in the Department. In 1972 the Directorate of Tourism was established independently.

Before the establishment of Madhya Pradesh Tourism Development Corporation (MPTDC) in May 1978, the Directorate of Tourism consisted of one Director, two Deputy Directors (One posted at Khajuraho), two Regional Tourist Officers, four Tourist Officers and thirty-four employees of class III & IV staff. Before this period, the Directorate was conducting affairs of Tourist Houses at Khajuraho, Mandu and Gwalior and a Youth Hostel at Bhopal, for which, separate staff was provided with a Manager at these places. After the establishment of MPTDC, the services of two

Regional Tourist Officers, four Tourist Officers and twenty-three employees of class III & IV were transferred to the Corporation. The Directorate of Tourism consists of one Director, one Deputy Director, nine employees of class III and two employees of class IV posts. Presently, the Directorate of Tourism is also managing the Youth Hostel at Bhopal. In this way, the Directorate comprises of sixteen Officers and Clerks including of that staff posted at Youth Hostel at Bhopal. Apart from the staff mentioned above, twenty-four tourist accommodation services, ten vehicles, and four tourist offices were transferred to the MPTDC by the order of the Government.

Therefore, it is clear that gradually expansion have taken place in the organization so as to act more effectively body. This necessarily implies that the tourist influx must have increased in the State and for which the organization was geared up so as to cope up with the increasing demand.

TOURIST PLACES IN THE STATE

The State offers a variety of attractions for all kinds of tourists. Every district in the State have something to attract the tourists of different nature and taste. On the basis of the information received from different districts and places of the State, the Department of Tourism, Government of India and the Directorate of Tourism, Madhya Pradesh, have documented one hundred twenty-five places which have potential for tourists attraction. Out of these one hundred twenty-five tourist places, sixteen major tourist places have been taken into account for the development because these places have the inflow of foreign tourists besides domestic tourists, while the others are popular among the domestic tourists only. A category-wise classification of these sixteen major tourist places is given below:

Category	*Name of the Places*
Historical & Archaeological	1. Gwalior
	2. Khajuraho
	3. Mandu
	4. Orchha

(*Contd.*)

Category	*Name of the Places*
	5. Sanchi-Udaigiri-Gyaraspur
Natural Setting	6. Baster
	7. Marble Rocks
	8. Pachmarhi
Religious	9. Chitrakoot
	10. Amarkantak
	11. Maheshwar
	12. Onkareswar
	13. Ujjain
Wildlife	14. Bandhavagarh National Park
	15. Kanha National Park
	16. Shivpuri National Park.

4

Employment Potential of Tourism in the State

Tourism is a 'labour-intensive service industry', and provides direct and indirect employment to a large segment of population. Several types of business firms, such as hotels, motels, restaurants, travel agents, tour operators, gift shops, transporters, earn bulk of tourist dollars. Various other secondary or allied business firms, for instance, construction firms, suppliers of food and beverages, taxi-drivers, photographers, hair-dressers, doctors also benefit out of it. Besides this there are a large number of specialist personnel required such as accountants, house-keepers, cooks, waiters, and entertainers who, in turn, need even large number of semi-skilled and unskilled workers such as chamber-maids, porters, kitchen staff and others. Thus, it is clear that tourism has been considered is an important factor in combating unemployment at the national and state level.

The State economy is composition of several factors, one of which is tourism. The principal area of its effect is the increase in opening the avenues for employment opportunities. This is, in fact, in relation to the expansion of local consumption area with a tourist centre as its central point. The present chapter deals with an important aspect of state economy that is impact of tourism in providing employment opportunities. No economy can survive unless it has adequate employment potential, and this can be achieved through:[1]

(a) expansion of local economic activities;
(b) increase in local production capacity;
(c) increase in local consumption due to the development of area;
(d) increase in local market due to increase in number of tourists arrivals, and
(e) increase in secondary sectors of local economy duly affected by the external factors or 'E' like tourism.

Tourist influx gives a boost to the economic activities of that particular area. These increased economic activities can be compared with those of areas which donot provide any tourist attraction to show that this has an impact on employment opportunities. An external factor like tourism affects the employment potential in two ways:

(a) it increases and expands—that is, qualitatively and quantitatively—the activities of producing sectors of the local economy, which further enhances local producing capacity, and this in turn, results in expanding the local employment potential; and
(b) it generates additional consumption capacity which requires additional employment in local producing sectors.

The employment opportunities in area economy can be direct or indirect in nature. Direct jobs are generated, such as those of hotel entrepreneurs, workers at resorts, guides, and in transport and handicraft industries. In addition to the usual things the tourist buys, mostly handicraft products, embroideries and brocades, potteries and brasswares, ornaments and artistic articles whicn have much greater appeals to the tourists. The expenditure of those directly employed in the tourist industry creates indirect jobs in hotels. These jobs are also attributed to the tourist industry, which is mainly reflected in increased employment opportunities in the construction industry, resulting from an expansion of tourism. Those indirectly employed in tourist industry create employment in other sectors of the industry through demand for goods and services. To sustain this additional demand, more people are required/employed in production of those goods and services. The cycle of increased income and employment continues at declining rate, until it is exhausted. This phenomenon is due to employment multiplier effects.[2]

A question can be raised as to whether tourism can become an industry with an opening of employment opportunities in organized and unorganized sectors. The answer is strongly in the affirmative. Tourism has the capacity of opening up avenues for providing employment in the various sub-sectors of the economy in the state. The above-mentioned form of employment opportunities gives to variance so far as organized sectoral economy is concerned. It can be explained on the basis of Fig. 4.1 and Fig. 4.2.

Fig. 4.1 and Fig. 4.2 of organized and unorganized sectors do not bring out properly the importance of employment opportunities created by tourist industry in the State. The Government attention to this industry, as a creator of employment, can only be drawn if we correctly assess the role of tourism in enhancing and strengthening the avenues of employment from all considerations, which can be elaborated with the help of the models (Fig. 4.3, Fig. 4.4 and Fig. 4.5).

The model consisting of 3 parts in this portion of the chapter is in fact designed to illustrate the impact of external factors like tourism on the State and sectoral economy, with reference to employment opportunities.

Model 1 Impact of Local Consumption Multiplier (LCM) on the State Economy with special reference to Employment Opportunities

This part of the model explains the impact of Local Consumption Multiplier on employment opportunities when it is affected by external factors or 'E' like tourism. There are 5 factors that affect Local Consumption Multiplier:

(i) The local consumption market of an area is stimulated by additional arrival of foreign tourists. The demand for luxury and essential goods increases due to additional influx of tourists. When the tourist season

Fig. 4.1: TOURISM AS AN ORGANISED SECTOR OF THE STATE ECONOMY

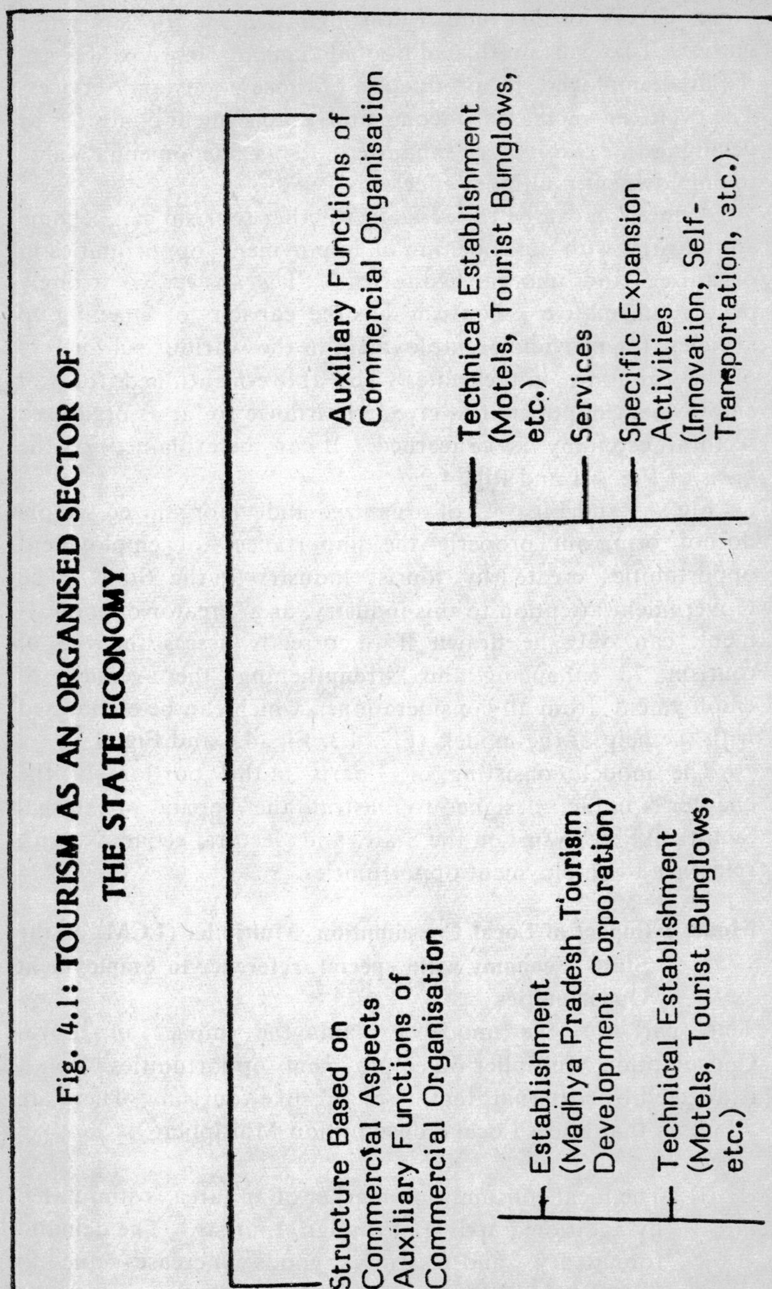

Fig. 4.2: TOURISM AS AN UN-ORGANISED SECTOR OF THE STATE ECONOMY

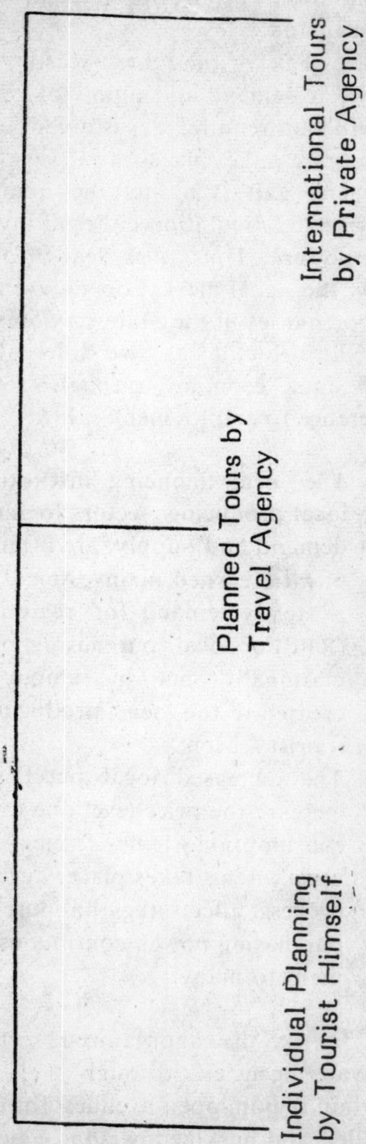

starts in that area, the economic activities (production, consumption and distribution) of the market aim to cope with the tourist influx. This process gives stimulation to local producing sectors (LPS) to meet the demand.

(ii) At the peak of the tourist season, there appears a gap between demand and supply of goods or items because production requires a sustained effort while consumption may take place at a very short notice. This artificial gap is, in fact, the quantum of money that may be in circulation either in investment or in hiring manpower. Thus, it is clear through this factor as to how the local market opens avenues for employment opportunities in the State economy.

(iii) The third factor has two different bases in sustaining the State economy through tourism with special reference to employment:

(a) The local financing institutions, while financing local producing sectors to meet the gap between demand and supply, are often affected by the profit ratio earned in investment. Thus there appears a steady demand for regional purchasing power (RPP) or local purchasing power (LPP) which is marginally met by employment opportunities created in the local producing sectors during the tourist season.

(b) The increased local purchasing power tends to increase the price level due to increase in domestic consumption. Thus artificial increase in price of luxury items takes place, due to tourist influx. This process affects regional purchasing power or local purchasing power continuously and offers employment to many.

(iv) So far as the unorganized sector is concerned, the private agencies, through their representatives in a certain region, open avenues for employment for many skilled and unskilled persons which is a sort of seasonal employment in nature. The tourist agencies keep in

Fig. 4.3

MODEL 1

IMPACT OF LOCAL CONSUMPTION MULTIPLIER ON THE STATE ECONOMY WITH SPECIAL REFERENCE TO EMPLOYMENT OPPORTUNITIES

1—Stimulation of LPS in relation to Tourism;

2—Artificial gap appears between Production & Consumption;

3—Demand for Local Regional Purchasing Power appears due to:

a—increase in Price Level;

b—artificial increase in Price Level due to tourist influx;

4—Additional influx of tourist increases the employment potential in Unorganized sector;

5—Unorganized employment potential minus Organized employment potential results in to increase Consumption Multiplier.

---

touch with local persons for providing necessary information about that region throughout the season. This can be considered a basis for providing employment opportunities in the region.

(v) This factor is one of the important parts in the model. It stresses the gap as created by the efforts made by government Agencies or Organized sectors to develop tourism as an industry in opening avenues for employment. This sort of artificial gap between organized and unorganized sectors creates 3 types of employment opportunities. They are: self employment; seasonal or offered employment and permanent employment. Thus these avenues of employment result in increasing local consumption multiplier (LCM) on the one hand and regional or local purchasing power (RPP or LPP) on the other.

Model 2 The State Economy (or 'a') in relation to External Factors, like tourism in the context of Employment

This part of the Model deals with the impact of external factors on the State economy with reference to employment. For convenience of the study, the model has been divided into three sub-parts.

(i) The first portion of the model deals with some economic and financial aspects like extra budgetary resources, which work as a supplementary financing agency in the unorganized sectors of the economy. This process requires additional taxation and, as soon as additional taxes are imposed, they increase non-budgetary resources. Thus it becomes essential to get

---

Fig. 4.4

MODEL 2

IMPACT OF EXTERNAL FACTORS, LIKE TOURISM ON THE STATE ECONOMY WITH REFERENCE TO EMPLOYMENT

1—Additional Budgetary Resources;

2—Excess Financing in Unorganized Sectors;

3—Additional Taxation;

4—Increase in Non-Budgetary Revenue;

5—Equilibrium between Foreign Exchange and National Currency;

6—Extra Demand for Goods;

7—Excess Supply;

8—Excess Demand for Manpower in Production Sector;

9—Meeting the need of Trained Manpower;

10—Extra influx of tourist requires additional suitable information;

11—Additional supply of Trained Manpower increases

an equilibrium position, between foreign exchange and national currency, on the basis of the total availability of foreign currency.

(ii) The second part elaborates the nature or impact of economic and financial factors on production and employment aspects. Owing to the effect of economic factors, the demand for essential and luxury items increases. The increased demand naturally requires extra supply of goods for which production has to be increased. Thus the demand for skilled and unskilled manpower increases in production sectors as well as in organized and unorganized sectors of the economy.

(iii) The last portion of the model deals with the supply of manpower—trained and untrained—to the tourist industry. A Corporation established by the government may require additional manpower to co-operate in the work. Trained manpower is required mainly in the catering, board and lodging and transportation services. The extra influx of tourists requires suitable and relevant information about a certain area. This additional information enhances supply of trained manpower in the tourist industry and hence it opens avenues for employment in the State.

Model 3 The Demand & Supply of Trained and Untrained Manpower in regard to Additional Tourist Influx

The Model explains how additional tourist influx opens avenues for employment in the tourist industry in the State. It consists of two economic factors as its basis: (i) sources of supply of trained and untrained manpower and (ii) demand for additional trained manpower.

These above-mentioned factors, when combined with additional tourist influx, result in an increase local producing sectors and consumption-production parallel (LPS and CPP) that further enhances local consumption multiplier (LCM).

CONCLUSION OF THE MODELS

The first Model describes two vital aspects of employment opportunities that enhance the avenues for employment in a

Fig. 4.5: DEMAND & SUPPLY OF TRAINED AND UN-TRAINED MAN POWER IN REGARD TO ADDITIONAL TOURIST INFLUX; MODEL – 3

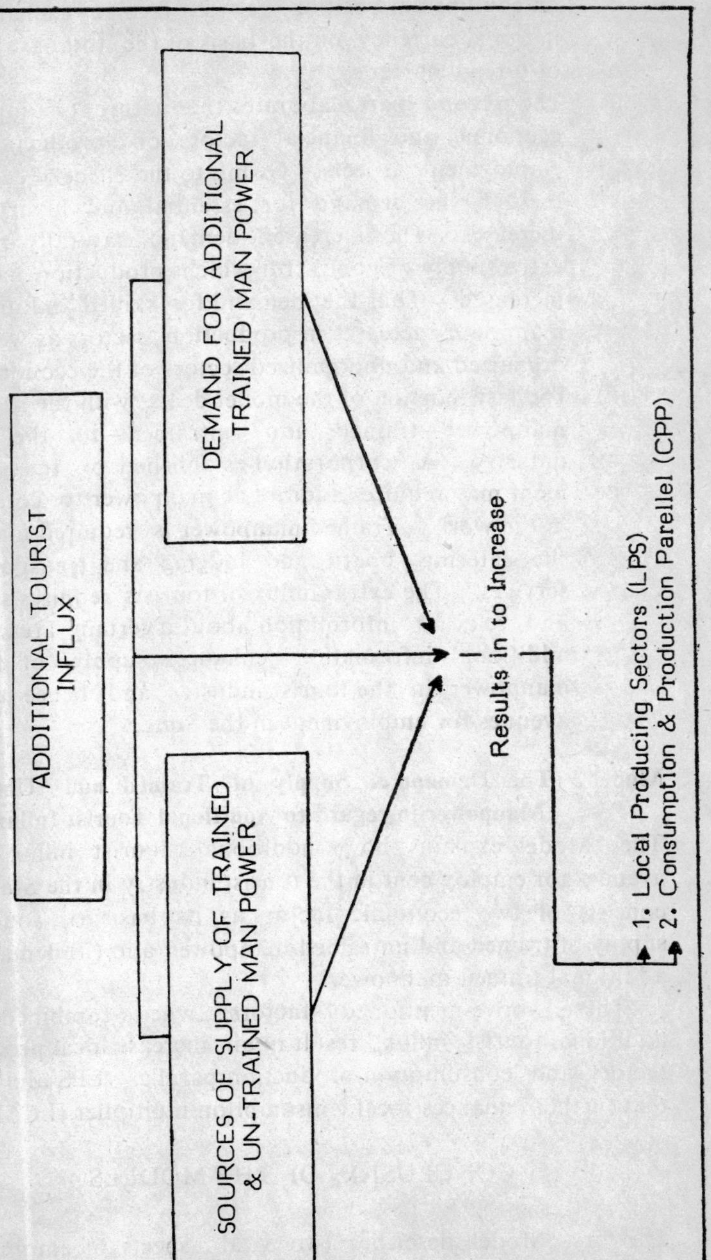

regional or State economy. It throws light on the expansion of local marketing facilities, local producing centres and regional purchasing power, which necessarily requires supply of additional manpower. The traditional concept regards tourism as an industry enhancing seasonal employment, but the first part of the model emphasizes the importance of this industry as a permanent field open for employment. During the tourist season, self-employed manpower or government employed manpower increases the local consumption multiplier in a regional economy.

The second part of the Model lays emphasis on budgetary investment for goods and manpower, and the capacity of the market to supply additional manpower, which increases the supply of trained and untrained manpower.

The last part describes the relationship with tourist influx which works as a balancing force between expanded sources of demand and supply of manpower, which further increases consumption and production parallel (CPP) and local producing sectors (LPS).

ANALYSIS OF DATA

In calculating the role of tourism in combating the unemployment in the State, the following points are to be noted:

(a) Those mainly employed in servicing the tourists are rarely distinguished at present from others employed in the similar activities but not connected with tourism and with other catering activities in official statistics. Similarly, employment in various forms of transport is shown, irrespective of its relationship with tourism and employment; the smaller sectors such as travel agencies is usually not enumerated separately.

(b) It is also seen that statistics of employment covers only employees and not others working as employers or self-employed. Tourist services are provided by many small units and they represent hardly a significant portion of the total manpower.

(c) Most of the tourist activities are seasonal. The number, employed in it, varies a great deal in peak and lean periods of the year.

Keeping in view the factors mentioned above, this study reveals the role, extent and scope of the tourist industry in solving the unemployment problem in the State. The statistical information given in support of the analysis has been collected from 16 important tourist centres (where inflow of foreign and domestic tourists occurs) and from available official sources. As this industry is not developed so far, no reliable statistical information is available about actual number of persons employed in the tourist industry either directly or indirectly. In the available State official sources, the tourist sector has not been accorded any special place of importance and, therefore, a proper estimate cannot be given about the actual number of establishments or the number of persons working in it; the number of persons working in hotels and restaurants out of the total working population and the employment opportunities available in the tourist industry. The same thing can be said regarding the transportation sector. An evaluation of the contribution of tourism towards providing employment in the State has been made here, on the basis of the available information from 16 major tourist destinations[3] and official and private agency publications.[4]

On the basis of the information from these sources regarding employment opportunities in tourist sector in the State, it can be stated that out of every hundred employed persons, twenty persons are employed in the tourist industry—both directly and indirectly.

The Table 4.1 indicates the total number of establishments and persons employed in them and the number of persons working in various sub-sectors of the establishment in the State.[5]

The Table 4.1 reveals that the total number of establishments in 1980 were 1,59,794 out of which 14,682 were restaurants and hotels, and 3353 were transport undertakings. The total number of persons employed in all the establishments in 1980 were 91,000, out of which 27,000 were employed in restaurants and hotels and 25,000 in transport undertakings in the State. On the basis of earlier growth, it is estimated by the Indian Labour Bureau, Ministry of Labour, that by 1984 the total number of establishments like restaurants and hotels would increase upto 17,982 while through these establishments

TABLE 4.1

Year	*Total Number of*		*Restaurants and Hotels*		*Transportation Sector*	
	Establishments	*Emp. ('000)*	*No. of Establishments*	*Emp. ('000)*	*Number of undertakings*	*Emp. in number*
1980	1,59,794	91	14,682	27	3353	25,000
1981	1,65,204	93	15,366	28	3392	25,028
1982	1,71,618	95	16,050	29	3420	25,346
1983	1;79,232	97	16,987	30	3489	25,864
1984	1,87,550*	99	17,982	31	3542	26,243

*Estimated.

the total number of persons able to get job opportunities may be about 31,000. In the same year (1984) the number of transport undertakings would increase to 3542 in which the total number of persons who would get employment are estimated at 26,243. The overall increase in establishments between 1980 to 1984 would amount to 3300 in restaurants and hotels and 189 in the transport sector. The total increase in employment would amount to 3000 in restaurants and hotels, and 1243 in transport undertakings. This increase indicates that on an average, one job increases in restaurants and hotels, and seven in the transport undertakings.

The Table 4.2 depicts the total employment in restaurant and hotels and transport undertakings and total number of persons actually working in tourist industry on the basis of the result drawn in the preceding part of the analysis.[6]

It is clear from the table that the total employment in restaurants and hotels in the State amounted to 58,000 persons during the period 1980-84. On the basis of the information

TABLE 4.2

Year	*Total no. of persons employed in rest. and hotels ('000)*	*20 per cent of Col. (ii)*	*Total no. of persons working in transport undertakings (in nos.)*	*20 per cent of Col. (iv)*
(*i*)	(*ii*)	(*iii*)	(*iv*)	(*v*)
1980	27	5400	25000	5000
1981	28	5600	25028	5006
1982	29	5800	25346	5070
1983	30	6000	25864	5173
1984	31	6200	26243	5250

drawn earlier, 20 per cent of 58,000 amounts to 11,600 persons working in restaurants and hotels in the tourist sector. The total number of persons employed in the transport sector during the period 1980-84, is estimated at 51243. Assuming 20 per cent of it, the employment figure comes to 10,249 in tourist transport sector. Therefore, the total number of persons employed in the tourist sector would be 21,849 by 1984. The ratio of persons employed in the tourist sector with the total working population of the State (which has been estimated as 2,00,70,564 by the Directorate of Economics and Statistics)[7] worked out of 919 : 10,000 which indicates that out of 10,000 persons 919 persons are employed in the tourist sector directly and indirectly.

There has been an increase in investment in tourism by more than 90 per cent from 1980 to 1984.[8] But it is interesting to note that this investment has not shown any impact on employment statistics of tourism sector in the State.

The following Table 4.3 shows the aggregate increase in the number of establishments and employment (in per cent) of restaurants and hotels and transport undertakings in the tourist sector from 1980 to 1984.

TABLE 4.3

	Restaurants and Hotels	*Transport undertakings*
Establishments (increased by)	660	38
Employment (increased by %)	11.11%	4.97%

The table indicates that the aggregate increase in the tourist sector amounts to 660 establishments in restaurants and hotels and 38 establishments in transport undertakings from 1980 to 1984. But the employment has not increased in proportion to the increase in establishments. It is mainly because—(a) this sector of the economy has not been found to have developed properly in the regions of the state; (b) due to lack of proper policy and attention to the tourist industry by the government caused imbalances in implementation of development policy; and (c) the establishments, such as hotels and restaurants and transport undertakings of this sector, are mainly with the private sectors and a sort of rivalry remains, which cannot be termed as a fair and healthy competition—results is not providing for better employment opportunities and thus the employment has not increased proportionately. The number of persons employed in restaurants and hotels and transport undertakings works out to 660 and 249 respectively. The aggregate increase in employment in restaurants and hotels is 11.11 per cent during 1980-84 while during the same year transport sector recorded an increase of 4.97 per cent.

A detailed statistical information regarding the employment in the various establishments in the state is shown in the Table 4.4.

In the early part of the chapter, it was noted that tourism is a labour-intensive service industry, but due to lack of

TABLE 4.4: **Employment in Establishments and Sub-sectors, in the State—1980-84**

Year	*Total Number of*		*Shops*		*Commercial Establishment*		*Restaurants and Hotels*		*Transportation Sector*	
	Establishments (in Nos.)	*Employment**	*Establishments (in Nos.)*	*Employments**	*Establishments (in Nos.)*	*Employment**	*Establishments (in Nos.)*	*Employment**	*No. of undertakings*	*Employment (in Nos.)*
1980	1,59,794	91	1,22,998	41	22,114	23	14,682	27	3,353	25,000
1981	1,65,204	93	1,27,556	41	22,282	24	15,366	28	3,392	25,028
1982	1,71,618	95	1,33,118	42	22,450	24	16,050	29	3,420	25,346
1983	1,79,232	97	1,39,456	42	22,789	25	16,987	30	3,489	25,864
1984E	1,87,550	99	1,46,528	43	23,040	25	17,982	31	3,542	26,243

Source: Indian Labour Statistics 1978, Labour Bureau, Ministry of Labour, Government of India, Chandigarh/Simla, 1982, pp. 50-51.

Note: The figures of Transportation sector are not included in Total Number of establishments and employment.

* The employments figures for Number of Establishments such as—(a) Shops, (b) Commercial Establishments and (c) Restaurants and Hotels are in '000s.

E : The figures for the year 1984 are estimated.

governmental attention, it has failed to provide proper employment opportunities. The above mentioned analysis indicates it clearly. On the basis of the analysis, the following points becomes clear:

1. The ratio of investment is in ascending order, while employment ratio is in descending order. Therefore, there has been negative co-relation between employment and investment;
2. The ratio of increase in employment is either marginal or negligible;
3. Whatever increase has been in restaurants and hotels and transport undertakings, regarding employment and establishment, may be due to the external factor or 'E', that is, tourism; and
4. Owing to lack of government attention towards investment and lack of creation of employment, this industry is still dependent on private agencies even today for opening avenues of employment.

In another word, it may be stated that the tourist industry has become a quite neglected labour-intensive-industry in the State economy, due to lack of proper policy, attention and promotional activities on the part of the government and due to improper understanding between public and private sectors.

REFERENCES

1. *Proceedings of the Symposium on the Planning and Development of the Tourist Industry in the ECE Region*, United Nations, New York, 1976, pp. 116-52.
2. J.M S. Negi, *Tourism and Hoteliering—A World-Wide Industry*, Geetanjali Publishing House, New Delhi, 1982, p. 70.
3. These 16 major tourist places are Gwalior, Khajuraho, Mandu, Orchha, Sanchi, Baster, Bheraghat, Pachmarhi, Chitrakoot, Amarkantak, Maheshwar, Onkareswar, Ujjain, Bandhavgarh, Kanha and Shivpuri.
4. (a) *Pocket Compendium of Madhya Pradesh Statistics—1982*, Directorate of Economics and Statistics, Madhya Pradesh, Government Regional Press, Gwalior, 1984.

(b) S.P. Ahuja, and S.R. Saran, *Tourism in India—A Perspective to 1990*, The Institute of Economic & Market Research, New Delhi, December 1977.

(c) *Employment Potential of Tourism in India—Vol. III: Income and Employment Effects*, Tata Economic Consultancy Services, Bombay, August, 1982.

5. *Indian Labour Statistics 1978*, Labour Bureau, Ministry of Labour, Government of India, Chandigarh/Simla, 1982, pp. 50-51.
6. Ibid.
7. *Pocket Compendium of Madhya Pradesh Statistics—1982*, op. cit., p. ii.
8. (a) *Budget Estimate 1982-83, Vol. I, Financial Statement*, Government of Madhya Pradesh, 1982.

   (b) Ibid., 1983.

   (c) Ibid., 1984.

5

Financial Aspects of Tourism

Madhya Pradesh has traditionally a large and diversified field of tourist attraction. The States's art, its culture, its places of historical and religious interest have always attracted tourists—both domestic and foreign. This tourist attraction has also proved to be a source of revenue to the Central Government and also to the State. The visits of tourists to such religious and historical areas laid the foundation of tourist industry. The regional economy has thus a source of revenue that has contributed to the State exchequer. The tourists carry with them two-fold opportunities for advancement of trade and commerce:

(i) the increase of local production and local consumption which gives impetus to a micro unit of the economy, that is, the local area economy, and
(ii) earnings of revenue, both foreign and domestic, in relation to the cash invested by the tourists.

This additional contribution in the area or State economy naturally warrants the attention of the government for fostering the needs of the tourist industry on the one hand and providing auxiliary services to the tourists on the other. The organized efforts on the part of the government include, commercial activities and regulation of the tourist industry, keeping in view the development of the industry.

The trade and commerce of a region enhance the opportunities for better survival for population, if it has something to contribute in expanding the Local Production and balancing the Consumption and Production. This stimulates periodically the local market and adds further revenue to the State exchequer. The public revenue of the State is to be considered as a blue print to the government activities extended or to be extended in a particular area. So far as the tourist industry is concerned, tourism is a revenue earning industry involving every sector of the local economy. The tourist industry offers four sources of revenue to an area economy or to the State economy:

(i) Expansion of currency facilities which stimulate the local market (Sales proceeds);
(ii) Expansion of local investment facilities and credit facilities (Share capital);
(iii) Stimulation of local production (Market Revenue); and
(iv) Stabilizing a higher price level by stimulation of the market (Price Index—Additional Tax).

It can be stated that, of all the revenue contribution heads the State, the major increase in the exchequer is due to the enhancement of local marketing facilities and enhancement of local purchasing power. For example, the urbanization of Khajuraho has given additional revenue to the State. A question may arise as to whether National, State and Area Economies have any link due to tourism. The answer is strongly in the affirmative, because the area economy through its additional marketing facilities adds revenue to the State exchequer and, on the other side, it also helps to build up sectoral economy at the National level.

It is astonishing to note that tourism has received the attention of the government lately. To lay down the commercial infrastructure of this industry, the government ought to have taken the initiative. The commercial activities of tourism, on governmental basis, began in the State in 1978 with the establishment of the Madhya Pradesh State Tourism Development Corporation. But, so far as the tourism sector is concerned, it remains as a 'neglected revenue oriented industry' in the State.

DATA ANALYSIS

(i) Revenue and Expenditure Pattern

The statistical information regarding revenue and expenditure pattern was not available for the period before 1980. The data available about expenditure by the government for tourism and the revenue contribution to the State exchequer by tourism, are given in Table 5.1.[1]

TABLE 5.1: **Expenditure and Revenue Pattern**

(*Rs in '000s*)

Year	*Total Expenditure by Government on Different Heads*	*Expenditure on Tourism*	*Total Revenue Contribution by Different Heads to the State Exchequer*	*Revenue Contribution by Tourism*
1980-81 (Accounts)	1,02,57,651	2,453	1,13,47,149	60
1981-82 (Accounts)	1,11,48,016	1,368	1,34,40,571	46
1982-83 (Accounts)	1,32,83,730	5,219	1,51,61,436	7
1983-84 (Budget Estimate)	1,62,84,795	4,635	1,74,51,374	5
1983-84 (Revised Estimate)	1,66,27,912	5,400	1,86,24,245	5
1984-85 (Budget Estimate)	1,81,86,319	5,980	2,00,04,891	5

Source: Budget Estimate 1984-85, Vol. 1, Financial Statement, Government of Madhya Pradesh, 1984.

The trend of expenditure on tourism indicates an increase since 1980-81. It was Rs 24,53,000 in 1980-81, which was .024% of the total expenditure. The expenditure is estimated to be Rs 59,80,000 in 1984-85 which is 0.33% of the total expenditure for the year. This indicates an increase of 0.09% be ween 1980-81 to 1984-85.

The statistical analysis of revenue shows a decrease since 1980-81. In that year the total revenue contributed to the exchequer was Rs 60,000 which was 0.005287% of the total revenue. The contribution decreased in the subsequent year 1984-85 and it was about Rs 5,000, which was 0.000249% of the total revenue contributed by different heads to the State economy.

A detailed statistical information regarding the revenue and expenditure pattern is shown in Table 5.2 and Table 5.3.

(2) **Budgetary Provision Analysis**

The provision made by the government for the tourist industry utilizes a major portion of the governmental resources on establishment costs. The available figures point out an increase of expenditure on administration and information. The budget estimates show two sources of revenue and expenditure. They are: (i) Plan and (ii) Non-plan. The plan expenditure includes: (a) Tourism Information and Publicity; (b) Tourism Accommodation and (c) Tourist Centres, while non-plan includes: (a) Directicn and Administration and (b) Tourism Transport Service. However, it is noticeable from the tables given in support of the analysis that out of the total revenue of the Department of Tourism, 3 major items utilize more than 50 per cent of the total revenue. They are: (a) Direction and Administration, (b) Transport and (c) Information and Publicity. It is also interesting to note that a very small percentage of revenue is allocated to the actual infrastructural facilities to be provided at the tourist centres.

The Table 5.4 indicates the budgetary provision as made by the government.[2]

Non-Plan

As compared to budget estimate 1981-82, the revised estimate 1981-82 showed a decrease of Rs 8,000. The budget estimate

TABLE 5.2: **Statement of Expenditure**

(Rs in '000s)

Heads	1980-81 Accounts	1981-82 Accounts	1982-83 Accounts	1983-84 Budget Estimate	1983-84 Revised Estimate	1984-85 Budget Estimate
1	2	3	4	5	6	7
General Services	1,06.502 (1.038)	1,08,526 (0.973)	1,20,895 (0.910)	1,45,242 (0.892)	1,64,069 (0.987)	1,31,367 (0.722)
Stamps and Registration	8,572 (0.083)	12,121 (0.109)	12,377 (0.093)	32,443 (0.199)	60,748 (0.365)	70,767 (0.389)
State Excise	65,505 (0.638)	82,248 (0.738)	92,470 (0.696)	92,369 (0.567)	1,06,516 (0.640)	1,11,325 (0.612)
Sales Tax	38,920 (0.379)	45,149 (0.405)	53,736 (0.404)	56,388 (0.346)	62,136 (0.374)	62,786 (0.345)
Taxes on Vehicles	6,562 (0.064)	5,876 (0.054)	7,367 (0.056)	10,557 (0.066)	11,187 (0.067)	11,858 (0.065)

(Contd.)

1	2	3	4	5	6	7
Other Taxes and Duties on Commodities and Services	7,459 (0.073)	7,482 (0.067)	8,940 (0.067)	61,094 (0.375)	57,981 (0.350)	68,282 (0.375)
Interest payment and servicing of Debt	7,97,463 (7.786)	10,44,014 (9.365)	11,50,131 (8.658)	14,07,127 (8.642)	14,07,708 (8.466)	17,71,518 (9.743)
Stationery and Printing	38,567 (0.376)	53,470 (0.480)	26,299 (0.473)	62,862 (0.386)	64,590 (0.388)	65,760 (0.362)
Art and Culture	13,394 (0.130)	17,959 (0.161)	20,162 (0.152)	28,110 (0.173)	31,349 (0.188)	33,070 (0.182)
Information and Publicity	14,418 (0.130)	14,647 (0.131)	18,142 (0.136)	18,305 (0.112)	22,060 (0.133)	25,881 (0.142)
Civil Aviation	311 (0.003)	205 (0.002)	153 (0.001)	235 (0.001)	405 (0.002)	390 (0.002)
Roads and Bridges	3,90,233 (3.804)	5,29,245 (4.747)	5,88,403 (4.429)	5,59,574 (3.436)	6,86,541 (4.129)	7,55,850 (4.156)
Road and Water Transport Service	12,792 (0.126)	— —	— —	— —	— —	— —

Tourism	2,453 (0.024)	1,368 (0.012)	5,219 (0.039)	4,635 (0.028)	5,400 (0.032)	5,980 (0.033)
Grant-in-Aid and Contributions	3,32,491 (3.241)	3,13,144 (2.809)	3,98,812 (3.002)	3,82,351 (2.348)	3,85,549 (2.319)	4,22,759 (2.324)
Miscellaneous	84,22,009 (82.105)	89,12,562 (79.947)	1,07,80,624 (80.860)	1,34,23,503 (82.429)	1,35,61,673 (81.560)	1,46,48,726 (80.548)
Grand Total	1,02,57,651 (100.00)	1,11,48,016 (100.00)	1,32,83,730 (100.00)	1,62,84,795 (100.00)	1,66,27,912 (100.00)	1,81,86,319 (100.00)

Source: 1. Budget Estimate 1982-83, Vol. I, Financial Statement, Government of Madhya Pradesh, 1982.

2. Budget Estimate 1983-84, Vol. I, Financial Statement, Government of Madhya Pradesh, 1983.

3. Budget Estimate 1984-85, Vol. I, Financial Statement, (As laid before the Vidhan Sabha in March, 1984), Government of Madhya Pradesh, 1984.

Note: The figures in parenthesis indicate the expenditure on different heads by the Government as per cent of total expenditure.

TABLE 5.3: **Revenue Contribution to the Exchequer**

(*Rs in '000s*)

Heads	*1980-81 Accounts*	*1981-82 Accounts*	*1982-83 Accounts*	*1983-84 Budget Estimate*	*1983-84 Revised Estimate*	*1984-85 Budget Estimate*
1	*2*	*3*	*4*	*5*	*6*	*7*
Taxes on Income and Expenditure	7,48,705 (6.598)	7,86,980 (5.855)	8,73,110 (5.759)	9,55,868 (5.477)	9,72,468 (5.222)	10,28,294 (5.140)
Stamps and Registration Fees	1,90,100 (1.675)	2,87,283 (2.137)	3,01,434 (1.988)	3,32,100 (1.903)	3,42,700 (1.840)	3,63,500 (1·817)
Estate Duty	2,551 (0.022)	5,109 (0.038)	4,238 (0.028)	4,900 (0.028)	4,900 (0.026)	5,400 (0.027)
State Excise	5,26,400 (4.639)	6,84,114 (5.089)	8,04,716 (5.308)	7,70,000 (4.412)	8,69,000 (4.666)	9,29,800 (4.648)
Sales Tax	17,78,500 (15.673)	24,36,041 (18.124)	28,39,529 (18.729)	30,64,000 (17.557)	31,64,500 (16.992)	34,81,000 (17.401)
Taxes on Vehicles	3,06,930 (2.705)	2,87,074 (2.136)	2,98,317 (1.968)	3,76,300 (2.156)	4,15,200 (2.229)	5,02,000 (2.509)

Taxes on Goods and Passengers	2,79,100 (2.459)	3,96,727 (2.952)	4,60,564 (3.038)	5,08,700 (2.915)	5,50,100 (2.953)	6,05,700 (3.028)
Interest Receipts, Dividends and Profits	5,41,614 (4.773)	7,15,136 (5.322)	8,41,136 (5.548)	10,11,394 (5.795)	9,98,657 (5.362)	11,43,241 (5.715)
Stationery and Printings	21,755 (0.192)	18,187 (0.135)	19,557 (0.129)	25,850 (0.148)	22,196 (0.119)	23,721 (0.118)
Art and Culture	165 (0.001)	231 (0.002)	162 (0.001)	280 (0.002)	240 (0.001)	290 (0.001)
Information and Publicity	200 (0.001)	388 (0.003)	411 (0.002)	210 (0.001)	264 (0.001)	289 (0.001)
Roads and Bridges	12,945 (0.115)	16,297 (0.121)	32,526 (0.214)	32,627 (0.187)	43,100 (0.231)	47,400 (0.237)
Tourism	60* (Neg. 1*)	46 (Neg. 2*)	7 (Neg. 3*)	5 (Neg. 4*)	5 (Neg. 5*)	5 (Neg. 6*)
Grant-in-aid and Contributions	42,08,626 (37.089)	44,38,165 (33.021)	47,92,617 (31.610)	59,48,539 (34.086)	64,03,897 (34.385)	66,45,550 (33.220)

(Contd.)

1	*2*	*3*	*4*	*5*	*6*	*7*
Miscellaneous	27,29,598 (24.055)	33,68,783 (25.064)	38,93,112 (25.678)	44,20,601 (25.332)	48,37,018 (25.972)	52,28,701 (26.173)
Grand Total	1,13,47,149 (99.999)	1,34,40,571 (99.999)	1,51,61,436 (99.999)	1,74,51,374 (99.999)	1,86,24,245 (99.999)	2,00,04,891 (99.999)

Source: 1. Budget Estimate 1982-83, Vol. I, Financial Statement, Government of Madhya Pradesh, 1982.

2. Budget Estimate 1983-84, Vol. I, Financial Statement, Government of Madhya Pradesh, 1983.

3. Budget Estimate 1984-85, Vol. I, Financial Statement, (As laid before the Vidhan Sabha in March 1984), Government of Madhya Pradesh, 1984.

Note: The figures in parenthesis indicate the revenue contribution to the State exchequer by different heads as per cent of total revenue contribution.

Neg.: Negligible, whereas the actual percentage is given below:

Neg. 1* : 0.0005287
Neg. 2* : 0.0003422
Neg. 3* : 0.0000461
Neg. 4* : 0.0000286
Neg. 5* : 0.0000268
Neg. 6* : 0.0000249

TABLE 5.4

(*Rs in '000s*)

	Accounts 1980-81	*Budget Estimate 1981-82*	*Revised Estimate 1981-82*	*Budget Estimate 1982-83*
Non-Plan				
Direction and Administration	476	241	233	360
Tourist Transport Service	134	40	40	95
Total Non-Plan	610	281	273	455
Plan				
Tourist Information and Publicity	1,020	600	600	1,500
Tourist Accommodation	190	210	210	311
Tourist Centres	453	450	450	688
Total Plan	1,663	1,260	1,260	2,499
Grand Total	2,273	1,541	1,533	2,954

Source: Budget Estimate 1982-83 and Demands for Grants 1982-83, Government of Madhya Pradesh, 1982.

1982-83 as compared to revised estimate 1981-82 showed an increase of Rs 1,82,000 mainly due to the inclusion of Rs 1,50,000 for payment of grant to M.P. State Tourism Development Corporation towards expenditure on staff (Rs 1,00,000) and maintenance of vehicles (Rs 50,000).

Plan

As compared to sanctioned budget/revised estimate 1981-82, the budget estimate 1982-83 showed an increase of Rs 12,39,000. Important variations are given as below:

(a) Tourist Information and Publicity (Rs 9,00,000) due to more provision for tourist publicity;

(b) Tourist Accommodation (Rs 1,01,000) due to grant to M.P. State Tourism Development for maintenance of accommodation for tourists; and

(c) Tourist Centres (Rs 2,38,000) due to more provision as grant to local bodies for providing facilities to tourists.

The Table 5.5 indicates the Capital Outlay on Other Transport and Communication Services.[3]

TABLE 5.5

(*Rs in '000s*)

	Accounts 1980-81	*Budget Estimate 1981-82*	*Revised Budget 1981-82*	*Budget Estimate 1982-83*
Plan				
Tourism	5,629	6,599	6,599	8,189
Total	5,629	6,599	6,599	8,189

Source: Budget Estimate 1982-83 and Demands for Grants 1982-83, Government of Madhya Pradesh, 1982.

As it is clear from Table 5.3 that the capital outlay as compared to sanctioned budget/revised estimate 1981-82, showed an increase of Rs 15,90,000, due to greater provision for investment in the share capital of M.P. State Tourism Development Corporation (Rs 1,50,000) and for providing facilities to the tourists (Rs 2,50,000).

These two tables, (Table 5.2 and 5.3) clearly showed an increase in non-productive expenditure. The Table 5.6 shows the same trend of expenditure on non-productive items like establishment, publicity and transportation.[4]

Non-Plan

The revised estimate for 1982-83, shows an increase of Rs 3,00,000 as compared to the budget estimate for 1982-83. The increase is mainly due to sanction of larger subsidy to the M.P. State Tourism Development Corporation for meeting expenditure on establishment of divisional publicity offices.

The budget estimate for 1983-84 shows an increase of Rs 1,00,000 as compared to the revised estimate for 1982-83. The increase was due to larger provision for subsidy to the M.P. Tourism Corporation for meeting expenditure on establishment of divisional offices.

Plan

The revised estimate for 1982-83 shows an increase of Rs 13,51,000 as compared to the budget estimate for 1982-83.

TABLE 5.6

(*Rs in '000s*)

	Accounts 1981-82	*Budget Estimate 1982-83*	*Revised Estimate 1982-83*	*Budget Estimate 1983-84*
Non-Plan				
Direction and Administration	238	360	660	755
Tourism Transport Service	22	95	95	100
Total Non-Plan	260	455	755	855
Plan				
Tourism Information and Publicity	600	1,500	1,500	1,500
Tourism Accommodation	191	311	250	400
Tourist Centres	281	688	2,100	1,450
Total Plan	1,072	2,499	3,850	3,350
Grand Total	1,332	2,954	4,605	4,205

Source: Budget Estimate 1983-84 and Demands for Grants, 1983-84, Government of Madhya Pradesh, 1983.

The increase is mainly due to inclusion of greater provision for giving subsidy to local bodies to provide facilities to tourists.

The budget estimate for 1983-84 shows a decrease of Rs 4,70,000 as compared to the revised estimate for 1982-83, which was based on actual requirements.

The Table 5.7 shows the Capital Outlay on Other Transport and Communication Services for tourism.[5]

Plan

The revised estimate for 1982-83 shows an increase of Rs 7,24,000 as compared to the budget estimate for 1982-83, and the increase was due to inclusion of greater provision for facilities to tourists.

The budget estimate for 1983-84 shows a decrease of Rs 4,63,000 as compared to the revised estimate for 1982-83, which was based on actual requirements.

The two Tables 5.4 and 5.6 and the Table 5.8 have one point of difference. The difference can be assessed as the change of policy and, for the first time, the State budget indicated the efforts of the government to provide basic facilities at tourist places on plan expenditure.[6]

TABLE 5.7

(*Rs in '000s*)

	Accounts 1981-82	*Budget Estimate 1982-83*	*Revised Budget 1982-83*	*Budget Estimate 1983-84*
Plan				
Tourism	10,437	8,181	8,915	8,533
Total	10,437	8,181	8,915	8,533

Source: Budget Estimate 1983-84 and Demands for Grants, 1983-84, Government of Madhya Pradesh, 1983.

Non-Plan

The revised estimate for 1983-84 shows an increase of Rs 7,000 as compared to the budget estimate for 1983-84. The increase was mainly due to provision for payment of arrears in the revised Choudhari Pay Scales.

TABLE 5.8

(*Rs in '000s*)

	Accounts 1982-83	*Budget Estimate 1983-84*	*Revised Estimate 1983-84*	*Budget Estimate 1984-85*
Non-Plan				
Direction and Administration	670	755	752	838
Tourism Transport Service	88	100	110	110
Total Non-Plan	758	855	862	948
Plan				
Tourism Information and Publicity	1,500	1,500	1,500	2,000
Tourist Accommodation	827	400	400	650
Tourist Centres	1,833	1,480	2,236	1,930
Total Plan	4,160	3,380	4,136	4,580
Grand Total	4,918	4,235	4,998	5,528

Source: Budget Estimate 1984-85 and Demands for Grants 1984-85, Government of Madhya Pradesh, 1984.

The budget estimate for 1984-85 shows an increase of Rs 86,000 as compared to the revised estimate of 1983-84. The increase is mainly due to provision for filling of vacant posts and normal growth of expenditure.

Plan

The revised estimate for 1983-84 shows an increase of Rs 7,56,000 as compared to the budget estimate for 1983-84. The increase is mainly due to inclusion of Provision for Grant-in-aid to the M.P. Tourism Corporation for the schemes proposed by the Government of India.

The budget estimate for 1984-85 shows an increase of Rs 4,44,000 as compared to the revised estimate for 1983-84. The increase is mainly due to greater Provision for Grant-in-aid to the M.P. Tourism Corporation for information and publicity.

The Table 5.9 depicts the Capital Outlay on Other Transport and Communication Services.[7]

TABLE 5.9

(*Rs in '000s*)

	Accounts 1982-83	*Budget Estimate 1983-84*	*Revised Budget 1983-84*	*Budget Estimate 1984-85*
Non-Plan				
Tourism	8,873	8,553	8,553	11,420
Total	8,873	8,553	8,553	11,420

Source: Budget Estimate 1984-85 and Demands for Grants 1984-85, Government of Madhya Pradesh, 1984.

It is clear from the table that the revised estimate for 1983-84 and the budget estimate for 1983-84 are equal.

Table 5.10: Statement of New Expenditure for the year 1984-85

(*Rs in '000s*)

Description	*Recurring*	*Non-Recurring*	*Total*
1	*2*	*3*	*4*
Grant-in-aid to Local Bodies and Special Area Development Authorities for basis facilities	—	1,550	1,550
Grant-in-aid for establishment of Statistical Cell	150	—	150
Grant-in-aid to M.P. State Tourism Development Corporation for role of Tourism in Economic Development and Urbanization by National Institute of Urban Affairs	200	—	200
Total	350	1,550	1,900
Capital outlay on other Transport and Communication **Services:**			
Investment in to Share Capital of M.P. State Tourism Development Corporation, Bhopal	—	9,270	9,270

(*Contd.*)

1	*2*	*3*	*4*
State share for Flood Lighting at Gwalior	—	300	300
State share for construction of Youth Hostel at Jabalpur	—	250	250
State share for construction of Dharmshala at Onkareshwar	—	300	300
Renovation of Rajgarh Palace—Khajuraho	—	200	200
Total	—	10,320	10,320

Source: Budget Estimate 1984-85 and Demands for Grants, 1984-85, Government of Madhya Pradesh, 1984.

TABLE 5.11: Demands for Grants

(*Rs. in '000s*)

Heads	*1980-81 Accounts*		*1981-82 Accounts*		*1982-83 Accounts*		*1983-84 Budget Estimate*		*1983-84 Revised Budget*		*1984-85 Budget Estimate*		
	Non-Plan	*Plan*	*Non-Plan*	*Plan*	*Non-Plan*	*Plan*	*Non-Plan*	*Plan*	*Non-Plan*	*Plan*	*Non-Plan*	*Plan*	*Total*
1	*2*	*3*	*4*	*5*	*6*	*7*	*8*	*9*	*10*	*11*	*12*	*13*	*14*
Revenue Section													
Direction and Administration	476	—	480	—	380	—	755	—	752	—	838	—	838
Tourist Information and Publicity	—	1,020	—	621	—	1,500	—	1,500	—	1,500	—	2,000	2,000
Tourist Transport Service	134	—	20	—	88	—	100	—	110	—	110	—	110
Tourist Accommodation	—	190	—	197	—	827	—	400	—	400	—	650	650
Tourist Centres	—	453	—	315	290	1,833	—	1,480	—	2,236	—	1,930	1,930
Total Revenue Section	610	1,633	500	1,133	758	4,160	855	3,380	862	4,136	948	4,580	5,528

(*Contd.*)

1	2	3	4	5	6	7	8	9	10	11	12	13	14
Capital Section													
Capital Outlay on other Transport and Communication Services: Tourism	—	5,629	—	10,437	—	8,873	—	8,553	—	8,553	—	11,420	11,420
Total Capital Account	—	5,629	—	10,437	—	8,873	—	8,553	—	8,553	—	11,420	—
Grand Total	610	7,262	500	11,570	758	13,033	855	11,933	862	12,689	948	16,000	16,948

Source: 1. Demands for Grants 1982-83, Government of Madhya Pradesh, 1982.

2. Demands for Grants 1983-84, Government of Madhya Pradesh, 1983.

3. Demands for Grants 1984-85, (As laid before the Vidhan Sabha in March 1984), Government of Madhya Pradesh, 1984.

TABLE 5.12: Detailed Account of Demands for Grants

(*Rs in '000s*)

Heads	*1980-81 Accounts*		*1981-82 Accounts*		*1982-83 Accounts*		*1983-84 Budget Estimate*		*1983-84 Revised Budget*		*1984-85 Budget Estimate*		
	Non-Plan	*Plan*	*Non-Plan*	*Plan*	*Non-Plan*	*Plan*	*Non-Plan*	*Plan*	*Non-Plan*	*Plan*	*Non-Plan*	*Plan*	*Total*
1	*2*	*3*	*4*	*5*	*6*	*7*	*8*	*9*	*10*	*11*	*12*	*13*	*14*
Revenue Section													
(a) *Direction and Administration*													
1. Directorate of Tourism:													
(i) Salaries:													
Pay of Officers	29	—	29	—	31	—	30	—	40	—	41	—	41
Pay of Establishment	34	—	32	—	36	—	50	—	80	—	117	—	117
Dearness Allowance	08	—	08	—	08	—	10	—	10	—	25	—	25
Additional D.A.	44	—	52	—	68	—	83	—	58	—	—	—	—
Interim Relief	04	—	08	—	08	—	10	—	05	—	10	—	10

(*Contd.*)

1	2	3	4	5	6	7	8	9	10	11	12	13	14
Medical charges	03	—	04	—	05	—	06	—	06	—	06	—	06
Leave Travel Concession	—	—	—	—	—	—	01	—	01	—	01	—	01
Other Allowances	04	—	03	—	04	—	05	—	05	—	10	—	10
Total (i)	126	—	136	—	160	—	195	—	205	—	200	—	200
(ii) Travel Expenses	7	—	10	—	14	—	10	—	10	—	10	—	10
Total (ii)	7	—	10	—	14	—	10	—	10	—	10	—	10
(iii) Office Expenses: Service Postage and Telegram	—	—	10	—	3	—	2	—	5	—	5	—	5
Telephone charges	—	—	6	—	32	—	30	—	35	—	38	—	38
Furniture and other office equipment	—	—	10	—	6	—	5	—	6	—	6	—	6
Books and Periodicals	—	—	5	—	3	—	2	—	3	—	3	—	3

Electricity and Water charges	—	—	5	—	4	—	3	—	5	—	5	—	5
Liveries	—	—	5	—	7	—	6	—	8	—	8	—	8
Stationery and Printing of Forms	—	—	10	—	3	—	2	—	3	—	5	—	5
Other contingencies	71	—	18	—	22	—	20	—	35	—	30	—	30
Total (iii)	71	—	69	—	80	—	70	—	100	—	100	—	100
(iv) Rent, Rates, and Taxes/Royalty	32	—	25	—	26	—	25	—	37	—	38	—	38
Total (iv)	32	—	25	—	26	—	25	—	37	—	38	—	38
(v) Grant-in-aid Staff Subsidy to M.P. Tourism Development Corporation	240	—	240	—	100	—	455	—	400	—	490	—	490
Total—(a)	476	—	480	—	380	—	755	—	752	—	838	—	838

(Contd.)

1	2	3	4	5	6	7	8	9	10	11	12	13	14
(b) *Tourist Information and Publicity*													
Advertising, Sales and Publicity	—	—	—	—	—	—	—	—	—	—	—	—	—
Grant-in-aid to M.P.T.D.C. for Information and Publicity	—	1020	—	621	—	1500	—	1500	—	1500	—	2000	2000
Total (b)	—	1020	—	621	—	1500	—	1500	—	1500	—	2000	2000
(c) *Tourist Transport Service* Operation of Tourist Coaches, Taxes, etc. for facility of tourists													
Wages	12	—	10	—	—	—	—	—	—	—	—	—	—
Rents, Rates, Taxes and Royalty	—	—	—	—	—	—	—	—	—	—	—	—	—

Grant-in-aid to M.P.T.D.C. for Maintenance of Tourist Vehicles	100	—	120	—	50	—	50	—	50	—	50	—	50
Motor Vehicles	22	—	20	—	38	—	50	—	60	—	60	—	60
Other charges	—	—	—	—	—	—	—	—	—	—	—	—	—
Total (c)	134	—	150	—	88	—	100	—	110	—	110	—	110
(d) *Tourist Accommodation*													
(i) Salaries:													
Pay of Officers	—	12	—	12	—	—	—	—	—	—	—	—	—
Pay of Establishment	—	2	—	1	—	—	—	—	—	—	—	—	—
Dearness Allowance	—	1	—	1	—	—	—	—	—	—	—	—	—
Additional D.A.	—	2	—	2	—	—	—	—	—	—	—	—	—
Medical charges	—	—	—	—	—	—	—	—	—	—	—	—	—
Leave Travel Concession	—	—	—	—	—	—	—	—	—	—	—	—	—
Other Allowances	—	1	—	1	—	—	—	—	—	—	—	—	—
Total (i)	—	18	—	17	—	—	—	—	—	—	—	—	—

(*Contd.*)

1	2	3	4	5	6	7	8	9	10	11	12	13	14
(ii) Travel Expenses	—	—	—	2	—	—	—	—	—	—	—	—	—
(iii) Office Expenses:													
Service Postage and Telegram	—	—	—	2	—	—	—	—	—	—	—	—	—
Telephone charges	—	—	—	4	—	—	—	—	—	—	—	—	—
Furniture and other Office Equipment	—	—	—	1	—	—	—	—	—	—	—	—	—
Books and Periodicals	—	—	—	2	—	—	—	—	—	—	—	—	—
Electricity and Water charges	—	—	—	7	—	—	—	—	—	—	—	—	—
Liveries	—	—	—	2	—	—	—	—	—	—	—	—	—
Stationery and Printing of Forms	—	—	—	1	—	—	—	—	—	—	—	—	—
Other contingencies	—	22	—	3	—	—	—	—	—	—	—	—	—
Total (iii)	—	22	—	24	—	—	—	—	—	—	—	—	—

(iv) Grant-in-aid: Grant-in-aid to M.P.T.D.C. for running tourist accommodation	—	150	—	155	—	627	—	400	—	400	—	650	650
Total (d)	—	190	—	196	—	827	—	400	—	400	—	650	650
(e) *Tourist Centres*													
(i) Grant-in-aid: Grant for construction of Approach road upto Dhuadhar in Bheraghat	—	—	—	—	—	—	—	—	—	—	—	—	—
Grant for construction of Approach road and day shelter in Chitrakoot	—	—	—	—	—	—	—	—	—	—	—	—	—
Repairs and renovation of Sign Boards in Pachmarhi	—	—	—	—	—	—	—	—	—	—	—	—	—

(*Contd.*)

1	2	3	4	5	6	7	8	9	10	11	12	13	14
Providing facilities of tented accommodation at Kanha	—	—	—	—	—	—	—	—	—	—	—	—	—
Grant to M.P.T.D.C. for tourist entertainment	—	267	—	—	—	—	—	150	—	906	—	150	150
Grant-in-aid to Local Institutions for providing tourist facilities	—	161	—	212	—	1833	—	1300	—	1300	—	1550	1550
Grant for Flower Valley and Snake Park	—	—	—	—	290	—	—	30	—	30	—	30	30
Grant-in-aid to M.P. Tourism Development Corporation for establishment of Office	—	—	—	—	—	—	—	—	—	—	—	200	200
Total (i)	—	428	—	212	290	1833	—	1480	—	2236	—	1930	1930

(ii) Minor Works:													
Development of Plaza at Khajuraho	—	—	—	—	—	—	—	—	—	—	—	—	—
Construction of Hotel at Khajuraho	—	25	—	25	—	—	—	—	—	—	—	—	—
Tourist Entertainment	—	—	—	—	—	—	—	—	—	—	—	—	—
Original Minor Works	—	—	—	—	—	—	—	—	—	—	—	—	—
Annual repairs, maintenance of buildings not borne on P.W.D. Books	—	—	—	—	—	—	—	—	—	—	—	—	—
Establishment of Recreation Centre at Khajuraho	—	—	—	78	—	—	—	—	—	—	—	—	—
Repairs and Furnishing of Tourist Bunglow at Mandla	—	—	—	—	—	—	—	—	—	—	—	—	—
Land Scaping at Bheraghat	—	—	—	—	—	—	—	—	—	—	—	—	—
Total (ii)	—	25	—	103	—	—	—	—	—	—	—	—	—

(*Contd.*)

1	2	3	4	5	6	7	8	9	10	11	12	13	14
(iii) Other charges: Purchase of Elephants at Kanha National Park	—	—	—	—	—	—	—	—	—	—	—	—	—
Total (e)	—	453	—	315	—	—	—	—	—	—	—	—	—
(f) *Tribal Areas Sub-Plan*: Normal Plan Scheme	—	—	—	—	—	—	—	—	—	—	—	—	—
Total Revenue Section	610	1663	500	1133	758	4160	855	3380	862	4136	984	4580	5528
Capital Section													
(i) Investment in Share Capital of Tourism Development Corporation	—	4600	—	8981	—	8478	—	7920	—	7920	—	9270	9270
(ii) Major Works: Acquisition of land and property at Pachmarhi and other tourist centres	—	—	—	—	—	—	—	—	—	—	—	—	—

Development of Regional Tourist Centres	—	—	—	—	—	—	—	—	—	—	—	—	—
Wayside amenities—Construction of Six Cafeteria, Landscaping and furnishing	—	—	—	—	—	—	—	—	—	—	—	—	—
Construction of approach road upto temples in Khajuraho	—	53	—	—	—	—	—	—	—	—	—	—	—
Flood Lighting at Bheraghat	—	—	—	478	—	200	—	225	—	225	—	300	300
Grant-in-aid to Local Institutions for providing Tourist Facilities	—	694	—	978	—	—	—	—	—	—	—	—	—
Water Supply in Bandhavgarh	—	113	—	—	—	—	—	133	—	113	—	50	50
Expenditure on approach road and road lighting to Orchha	—	47	—	—	—	—	—	—	—	—	—	300	300

(*Contd.*)

1	2	3	4	5	6	7	8	9	10	11	12	13	14
Construction of Staff Quarters	—	122	—	—	—	—	—	—	—	—	—	200	200
Contribution of State Govt.'s share towards Construction of Tourist Village at Shivpuri	—	—	—	—	—	200	—	275	—	275	—	750	750
TOTAL CAPITAL SECTION	—	5629	—	10437	—	8873	—	8553	—	8553	—	11420	11420
GRAND TOTAL	610	7262	500	11570	758	13033	855	11930	862	12689	948	16000	16948

Source: 1. Demands for Grants 1982-83, Government of Madhya Pradesh, 1982.
2. Demands for Grants 1983-84, Government of Madhya Pradesh, 1983.
3. Demands for Grants 1984-85 (As laid before the Vidhan Sabha in March 1984); Government of Madhya Pradesh, 1984.

The budget estimate for 1984-85 indicates an increase of Rs 28,67,000 as compared to the revised estimate for 1983-84. The increase is due to greater provision for investment in the share capital of the M.P. Tourism Development Corporation (Rs 13,50,000) and major works for providing facilities to tourists, and construction of other works (Rs 15,17,000).

After the review and analysis of Budgetary Provision from the year 1980-81 to 1984-85 (Budget estimate), the statement of new expenditure for the year 1984-85 is given in the Table 5.10.[8]

A detailed statistical information regarding the budgetary provision is shown in the Table 5.11 and Table 5.12.

The present chapter reveals the following important points:

(a) The proportion of investment by the government in the sphere is not up to the requirement; rather, it is much less than the required;

(b) Owing to bureaucratic inconvenience and lack of commercial experience, the yields in this sector of the economy are virtually negligible. They are not proportionate to the investment;

(c) More than 50 per cent of the total expenditure goes on non-productive items, like Direction and Administration, Transport and Information and Publicity; and

(d) The tourism sector lacks strong governmental initiative and adequate finances for commercialising the sector, and hence it remains as a 'neglected revenue oriented industry' in the economy of Madhya Pradesh.

REFERENCES

1. (a) *Budget Estimate 1982-83, Vol. I, Financial Statement*, Government of Madhya Pradesh, 1982, pp. 1-17.
   (b) Ibid., 1983, pp. 1-17.
   (c) Ibid., 1984, pp. 1-17.
2. *Demands for Grants 1982-83*, (*Demand No. 37, Tourism*), Government of Madhya Pradesh, 1982, p. 11.

3. Ibid., p. 11.
4. *Demands for Grants 1983-84* (*Demand No. 37, Tourism*), Government of Madhya Pradesh, 1983, p. 11.
5. Ibid., p. 11.
6. *Demands for Grants 1984-85* (*Demand No. 37, Tourism*), (As laid before the Vidhan Sabha in March 1984), Government of Madhya Pradesh, 1984, p. 11.
7. Ibid., p. 11.
8. Ibid., p. 12.

6

An Overview

Tourism, both domestic and international, has rapidly won considerable recognition as an activity generating a number of social and economic benefits like promotion of national integration, and better international undertaking. It has created employment opportunities, removed regional disparities or imbalances, and augmented foreign exchange earnings. Hence it has redressed the balance of payments situation. It also tends to give support to local handicrafts, and cultural activities, both in rural and urban areas. Expenditure by tourists has a multiplier effect, and also generates considerable tax revenue for the government, both in the Central and State sectors. Today, the tourist industry, including the hotel business, is the second largest in the world, heading towards overtaking oil in the coming decade.

The present study is an inquiry to examine the role of tourism in a relatively backward economic region of the country, that is, the State of Madhya Pradesh, and the extent of its contribution to the economy. During the study, further queries cropped up, like the dominance and scope of the role played by tourism in the State economy and the extent of that scope. The major areas of study are the employment potential and financial aspects of tourism.

The value of tourism to the national economy is measured generally in terms of its contribution to the national income, employment and tax revenue accruing to the government.

When we perceive the contribution of India's tourism to the national economy, two important points become clear. They are presented below:

(i) Between 1951 and 1981, the compound growth rate of tourist arrivals in the country was 14 per cent as against the world average of 8.2 per cent and, with this, India's share of the world tourist traffic went up five fold, but it was still a meagre 0.29 per cent;

(ii) There has been an uninterrupted growth in foreign exchange receipts since 1951. During the period 1951-81, India achieved a compound growth rate of 16.2 per cent in foreign exchange earnings as against the world average of 13.5 per cent.

These results indicate that the growth rate and progress of the tourist industry is not proper. The main causes behind it can be the lack of a comprehensive policy for development, and unbalanced co-ordination between public and private agencies together with government sectors. To some extent, the planning process as it stands at present, is also responsible for not making integrated plans to promote tourism in the country. From this, it is clear even to a layman that organized efforts to develop the tourist industry are still negligible.

A review of available literature on different aspects of tourism, has been briefly summarised. But it is interesting to note that a number of studies on the economic aspects of tourism has been conducted at international and national levels, and very few of the investigations are directed at regional and local levels. The studies at regional and local levels have not included the impact of employment and financial aspects at micro-level unit. The present study, therefore, may help to determine the contribution made by the tourism sector to the regional economy and then to the State economy.

The term 'economy' carries a definite meaning. In fact, the economy is a cumulative effect of various activities performed horizontally and vertically. Horizontal activities are known as the sectoral economic activity while vertical activities are known as regional, or the State or National or International economy. It is difficult to locate the actual nature of the State economy, which is considered a micro unit of the national economy. In the present study, an effort has been made to find out the regional imbalances in the State economy. Tourism also enhances the marketing aspect of the economy within a region. Tourist activity within a region can be derived by subtracting international economy plus regional marketing facilities from national economy plus regional purchasing power and, therefore, the State economy with special reference to tourism becomes a sectoral economy in the national sphere.

The models, described in Chapter 3 in two parts—A and B, reveal the impact of tourism on the regional economy of the State. The first part, that is, portion A, consists of seven sub-parts, and shows how the regional economy is gradually affected by the constant factor, 'E', that is, external factors like tourism. This 'E' factor motivates, extends and affects the local consumption activities, increases the local production, and then results in to convert local consumption multiplier as its own square. Part B of the model, which has two sub-parts, depicts that tourist economy is the derivation of components of price index subtracted from tourist facilities and number of tourist arrivals, which further results in an increase in local consumption multiplier.

By reviewing the different Five-Year Plan documents for the various activities to promote tourism in the State, it becomes clear that at this level, no sustained and proper efforts have been made to develop the tourist industry as a positive factor of the economy. Although, on the other hand, the Directorate of Tourism and Madhya Pradesh State Tourism Development Corporation, two administrative and commercial units were established in the State in 1961 and 1978 respectively, to provide necessary facilities to promote tourism through an integrated approach, at regional and State level. Their efforts in this direction do not indicate a good picture of the progress. Therefore, it is necessary that these organized units should co-operate with public and private sectors of the economy to create such conditions as are favourable for development.

Tourism brings in its wake a spurt of employment opportunities, and employs a large number of people—both directly and indirectly. It is for this reason that tourism is regarded as a labour-intensive service industry. It is also considered a valuable source of employment, particularly for those areas where seasonal unemployment and underemployment often exist. Chapter 4 deals with the role of tourism as a creator of employment in the State economy. The models constructed in three parts in this chapter indicate the types of avenues for employment that are available through the constant and steady effect of external factors or 'E', like tourism. The necessity of these models resulted when it was difficult to locate the nature and types of employment that tourism can provide in the State due to lack of statistics. Estimates of the impact of tourism on employment obtained in the present study show that tourism is not a significant sector of the State economy because its total contribution is towards national economy through foreign exchange.

The tourist activities in the tourist areas also appear insignificant because its estimated share in the total employment works out to about 1 per cent during 1980-84. The figure which shows the ratio of increase in employment is either marginal or negligible. The total number of jobs, created by tourism in restaurants and hotels and transport undertakings units is estimated about eight. One point also becomes clear through the analysis that, whatever increase there has been in restaurants and hotels and transport undertakings regarding employment, it is only due to extra influx of tourists or external factors like tourism. But due to lack of proper co-ordination between public and private agencies together with the government sector, tourism, which is considered a labour-intensive service industry, remains a neglected industry in the State economy.

Finances are considered, for any industry or economic activity, the backbone for development because finances stimulate the inflow of labour and outflow of extracted revenue. The financial aspects included in the study are: expenditure by the government towards tourism and the revenue contribution to the State exchequer from this industry, and budgetary provision made by the State government for the development of tourism annually. The expenditure by the government to develop this industry to earn foreign exchange, indicates an increase of .009 per cent between 1980-81 and

1984-85. This increase in expenditure for tourism is negligible, when we perceive it in the context of the total expenditure.

On the other side, the revenue contribution to the State exchequer by the tourism sector depicts an interesting point. The revenue contribution statistics show a decrease of .0005038 per cent from 1980-81 to 1984-85. The budgetary provision figures between 1980-81 and 1984-85 indicated an increase of expenditure by more than 50 per cent of the total provision made for tourism, on non-productive items like Direction and Administration, Transport and Information, and Publicity. Productive items through which the tourism sector can enlarge and enhance the economic activities for earning money and attracting more foreign tourists, have been allocated a small amount for development programmes. It is also interesting to note that, although this industry is commercialized on the government basis theoretically, it depends in practice for its development mostly on private agencies. Owing to lack of formulation of proper policy for financial allotment and the right ways to utilize the amount of investment, the tourist sector remains a neglected revenue-oriented industry in the State economy.

From the analysis above, it is clear that tourism development can become a positive factor for improving the economic condition of the State. For this purpose, some measures have to be adopted at national, State and then at regional levels. The following are the some of the important points to be observed in this respect:

(a) The State Government with the help of the Central Government should prepare a master plan for the development of tourism. The plan should be made in such a way that it would be able to develop the places where facilities already exist and simultaneously take up the development of new basis having significant tourist potential, which have not been exploited so far;

(b) In formulating a proper policy for planning, the State government should keep in view the following two points:

(i) the quantitative and qualitative targets in respect of number of tourists likely to visit the State and the estimated earnings from them and consequently the investment required for tourism development should be defined clearly in the draft plan, and

(ii) the volume, nature and sources of capital that has to be spent on development programmes and the terms and conditions on which that capital can be available easily should be given proper attention;

(c) As it is already known, data on tourism still leave much to be desired in terms of reliability and coverage. There are no proper data sources giving figures in the State; and the paucity of the data also creates difficulty in the construction of an input-output table for the tourism sector. It is, therefore, suggested that the State Government, with the help of the Central Government, should organize a project at regional and local levels to get the inter-industry picture with special reference to tourism;

(d) Special consideration must be given to recording the employment opportunity statistics, created by the tourist industry in the State. Also, employment possibilities should be recorded in every sector that works as an auxiliary industry to the tourist industry. Although some provision has been made by establishing a statistical cell at the State level for tourism in the proposed new expenditure plan for the year 1984-85, the success of this new unit will depend upon its working and performance;

(e) The State can also help in tourism development by conducting market research both overseas and within the country to provide guidelines to the private sector for development and promotion of tourism accordingly;

(f) A systematic effort should be made to collect statistics of domestic tourists duly classified into different categories and their respective interests broadly ascertained with a view to concentrating on the development of such areas of interest;

(g) The State budget provision made for this sector should be such that productive items are allocated more funds than non-productive items;

(h) Foreign exchange facilities should also be provided at important tourist centres to avoid inconvenience to tourists.

In this study an attempt has been made to measure the impact of tourism on the economy of Madhya Pradesh. Owing to limitations of data availability, no attempt could be made to estimate relevant multiplier coefficients for the tourists' expenditure in the State. This study is aimed at enhancing our understanding and measuring economic value of tourism in the State. Tourism as a 'mass consumption' phenomenon has been subjected to economic analysis because the demand created by tourism is to be met by the development of a new sector, the 'tourist industry'.

Bibliography

Adnur, P. *Integrated Tourism Development—Plan for Master City.* Indian Institute of Management, Bangalore, 1981.

Ahuja, S.P. & S.R. Saran. *Tourism in India—A Perspective to 1990.* The Institute of Economic and Social Research, New Delhi, 1977.

Allchin, F.R. *Cultural Tourism in India—Its Scope and Development.* Department of Tourism, Government of India, New Delhi.

Anand, M.M. *Tourism and Hotel Industry in India—A Study in Management.* Prentice-Hall of India Pvt. Ltd., New Delhi, 1976.

Archer, B.H. *Demand Forecasting in Tourism.* University of Wales Press, Cardiff, 1974.

——. *The Impact of Domestic Tourism.* University of Wales Press, Cardiff, 1973.

Archer, B.H., S. Shea and R. Vane. *Tourism in Gwyneed: An Economic Study.* Institute of Economic Research, University College of Wales, Bangor, 1974.

Bhatia, A.K. *Tourism in India—History and Development.* Sterling Publishers Pvt. Ltd., New Delhi, 1978.

——. *Tourism Development—Principles and Practices.* Sterling Publishers Pvt. Ltd., New Delhi, 1982.

Brown, A.J. & E.M. Burrows. *Regional Economic Problems—Comparative Experiences of Some Market Economics.* George Allen and Unwin, London, 1977.

Blaug, Mark. *The Methodology of Economics or How Economists Explain.* Cambridge University Press, Cambridge, 1980.

Bryden, John M. *Tourism and Development.* Cambridge University Press, Cambridge, 1973.

Burkart, A.J. *The Management of Tourism*. Heinemann, London, 1975.

Burkart, A.J. and S. Medlik. *Tourism: Past, Present and Future*. Heinemann, London, 1976.

Burnner, E. *Holiday Making and Holiday Trade*. Oxford University Press, London, 1945.

Cleverdon, R. *The Economic and Social Impact of International Tourism on Developing Countries*. The Economic Intelligence Unit Ltd., London, 1979.

Colley, G. *International Tourism Today*. Lloyds Bank Review, London, 1967.

Crampon, L.T. *An Analysis of Tourist Markets*. University of Colorado Press, Colorado, 1963.

——. *Development of Tourism*. University of Colorado Press, Colorado, 1963.

Davis, H.D. *Potentials for Tourism of Developing Countries*. Finance and Development, London, 1968.

Das, Nabagopal. *The Inaian Economy Under Planning*. The World Press Pvt. Ltd., Calcutta, 1972.

Donald, E. *Tourism Planning and Development Issues*. George Washington University, Washington, 1980.

——. *Tourism Marketing and Management Issues*. George Washington University, Washington, 1980.

Gearing Charles, E. *Planning for Tourism Development—Quantitative Approach*. Praeger Publisher Inc., New York, 1976.

Gray, H. Peter. *International Travel—International Trade*. Health Lexington Books, Lexington, 1970.

Hammarskjold, K. *Economics of Air Transport and Tourism*. I.C.A.O., Montreal, 1972.

Hanson, J.L. *Dictionary of Economics and Commerce*. English Language Book Society & MacDonald & Evans Ltd., London, 1969.

Henderson, D.M. *The Economic Impact of Tourism: Case Study in Greater Tayside*. Research Report No. 13, Tourism and Recreation Research Unit, University of Edinburgh, 1975.

Hunziker, W. *General Tourist Theory*. Zurich, 1942.

——. *Social Tourism, Its Nature and Problems*. Alliance Internationale de Turisme, Geneva, 1951.

Ian M.M. *The Geography of International Tourism*. Association of American Geographers, Washington, 1976.

John, M. Bryden. *Tourism and Development.* Cambridge University Press, London, 1973.

Kaiser, Charles F. and Larry E. Helber. *Tourism Planning and Development.* CBI Publishing Company, Inc., Boston, 1978.

Lawson, M. *Teaching Tourism—Education and Training in Western Europe—A Comparative Study.* Tourism International Press, London, 1975.

Lickorish, L.J. *Tourism and International Balance of Payments.* International Institute of Scientific Travel Research, Geneva, 1953.

——. *Tourist Promotion and Publicity Media.* National Institute of Scientific Travel Research, Geneva, 1953.

Lundberg, D. *The Tourist Business.* Cahners Books, Boston, 1974.

——. *International Travel and Tourism*, ICTA, New York, 1970.

Mathieson, A. & G. Wall. *Tourism-Economic Physical and Social Impact*, Longman Group Ltd., London, 1982.

McIntosh, R.W. *Tourism: Principles, Practices and Philosophies*, Grid Inc., Ohio, 1977.

Medlik, S. *Higher Education and Research in Tourism in Western Europe*, University of Surrey, Surrey, 1966.

——. *The Economic Importance of Tourism.* University of Surrey, Surrey, 1972.

——. *Organization of Tourism in Six European Countries.* University of Surrey, Surrey, 1966.

Mitchell, F. *The Economic Value of Tourism in Kenya.* University of California, California, 1971.

——. *The Costs and Benefits of Tourism in Kenya.* Institute of Development Studies, Nairobi, 1968.

——. *The Impact of Tourism in National Income.* Institute of Development Studies, Nairobi, 1968.

Norval, A.J. *The Tourist Industry: A National and International Survey*, Issac Pitman & Sons Ltd., London, 1963.

Negi, J.M.S. *Tourism and Hoteliering—A World Wide Industry.* Gitanjali Publishing House, New Delhi, 1982.

Ogilvie, F.W. *The Tourist Movement—An Economic Study.*

Stapless Press, London, 1933.

Pearce, Sales J. *Travel and Tourism Encyclopaedia.* Blandfor, London, 1959.

Peters, M. *International Tourism.* Hutchinson, London, 1969.

Rae, P.W. *The Business of Travel.* Thomas Cook & Son, London, 1891.

Rakshit, G. *India's Fifth Plan—A Critical Assessment.* The World Press Pvt. Ltd., Calcutta, 1977.

Ram Acharya. *Civil Aviation and Tourism Administration in India.* National Publishing House, New Delhi, 1978.

Ramakar, J.G. *Tourism and Transport.* Scientific Commission of the Alliance International De Tourism, 1954.

Richards, G. *Tourism and the Economy.* University of Surrey, Surrey 1972.

Richardson, H.W. *Regional Economics: A Reader.* Macmillan & Co. Ltd., London, 1970.

Robinson, H. *A Geography of Tourism.* MacDonald and Evans, London, 1976.

Sainy, H.C. *India's Foreign Trade; Its Nature and Problems.* National Publishing House, New Delhi, 1979.

Schmoll, G.A. *Tourism Promotion.* Tourism International Press, London, 1977.

Schultze, C.L. *National Income Analysis.* Prentice-Hall Inc., Englewood Cliffs, New Jersey, 1965.

Selltiz, C., M. Jahoda, M. Deutsch, and S.W. Cook. *Research Methods in Social Relations.* Holt, Rinehart and Winston, Inc., New York, 1963.

Sen, S.R. *The Planning Machinery of India.* Planning Commission, Government of India, New Delhi.

Sessa, Alberto. *Tourism in Developing Countries.* Reprint from Manual on the Conservation, UNESCO, Paris, 1970.

Seth, P.N. *Successful Tourism Planning and Management.* Cross Section Publications, New Delhi, 1978.

Sigaux, G. *History of Tourism.* Leisure Art, London, 1966.

Singh, T.V., J. Kaur, and D.P. Singh. *Tourism Wildlife Parks Conservation.* Metropolitan Book Co. Ltd., New Delhi, 1982.

Steward, J.H. *Area Research—Theory and Practice.* Social Science Research Council, New York, 1950.

Thangamani, K. *Studies in Tourism Development Planning.*

Institute of Development Studies, Mysore University.

Titmuss, R.M. *Income Distribution and Social Change.* George Allen and Unwin Ltd.. London, 1963.

Vaughan, R. *The Economic Impact of Tourism in Edinburgh and Lothian Region.* Scottish Tourist Board, Edinburgh, 1977.

——. *The Economic Impact of Edinburgh Festival—1976.* Scottish Tourist Board, Edinburgh, 1977.

Wahab, C.R. *Tourism Marketing.* Tourism International Press, London, 1976.

Wahab, S. *Tourism Management.* Tourism International Press, London, 1975.

Waugh, R.E. *The American Traveller: Move Darkness than Light ?* Bureau of Business Research, University of Texas, Austin, 1962.

White, J. *History of Tourism.* Leisure Art, London, 1967.

Young, G. *Tourism-Blessing or Blight.* Penguin Books, Middlesex, U.K., 1973.

Young, P.V. *Scientific Social Surveys and Research.* Asia Publishing House, Bombay, 1960.

Yukic, T.S. *Fundaments of Recreation.* Harper Row, London, 1963.

OFFICIAL AND OTHER REPORTS

A Study of Seasonal Pattern of Tourist Movement in India. Statistics and Research Department, Department of Tourism, New Delhi.

Ad hoc Committee on Tourism. Department of Tourism, March 1963.

Budget Estimate 1982-1983, Vol. I, Financial Statement. Government of Madhya Pradesh, Bhopal, 1982.

Budget Estimate 1983-84, Vol. I, Financial Statement. Government of Madhya Pradesh, Bhopal, 1983.

Budget Estimate 1984-85, Vol. I, Financial Statement. Government of Madhya Pradesh, Bhopal, 1984.

Demands for Grants 1982-83. Government of Madhya Pradesh, Bhopal, 1982.

Demands for Grants 1983-84. Government of Madhya Pradesh, Bhopal 1983.

Demands for Grants 1984-85. Government of Madhya

Pradesh, Bhopal, 1984.

First Five Year Plan. Planning Commission, Government of India, New Delhi.

Fourth Five Year Plan. Planning Commission, Government of India, New Delhi.

Fifth Five Year Plan. Planning Commission, Government of India, New Delhi.

Indian Labour Statistics, 1978. Labour Bureau, Ministry of Labour, Government of India, Simla, 1982.

Pocket Compendium of Madhya Pradesh Statistics, 1982. Directorate of Economic and Statistics, Bhopal, 1984.

Report of the Estimates Committee. First Lok Sabha, Thirty-fourth Report, Ministry of Transport, Lok Sabha Secretariat, New Delhi.

Report of the Estimates Committee. Second Lok Sabha, Fifty-second Report (Action Taken Report), Ministry of Transport, Lok Sabha Secretariat, New Delhi.

Report of the Estimates Committee. Fourth Lok Sabha, Ninetieth Report, Ministry of Tourism and Civil Aviation, Department of Tourism, Lok Sabha Secretariat, New Delhi.

Report of the Estimates Committee. Fourth Lok Sabha, Hundred and Thirtieth Report (Action Taken Report), Ministry of Tourism and Civil Aviation, Department of Tourism, Lok Sabha Secretariat, New Delhi.

Report of the Estimates Committee. Fifth Lok Sabha, Fifty-fifth Report, Ministry of Tourism and Civil Aviation, Lok Sabha Secretariat, New Delhi.

Report of the Public Accounts Committee. Third Lok Sabha, Sixty-third Report, Ministry of Tourism and Civil Aviation, Department of Tourism, Lok Sabha Secretariat, New Delhi.

Report of the Public Accounts Committee. Fourth Lok Sabha, Twenty-fifth Report, Ministry of Tourism and Civil Aviation, Department of Tourism, Lok Sabha Secretariat, New Delhi.

Report of the Public Accounts Committee. Fourth Lok Sabha, Sixty-fifth Report, (Action Taken Report), Ministry of Tourism, and Civil Aviation, Department of Tourism, Lok Sabha Secretariat, New Delhi.

Report of the Public Accounts Committee. Fourth Lok Sabha, Seventieth Report (Action Taken Report), Ministry of Tourism and Civil Aviation, Department of Tourism, Lok Sabha Secretariat, New Delhi.

Report of the Committee on Public Undertakings. Fourth Lok Sabha, Seventeenth Report, India Tourism Development Corporation Limited, Ministry of Tourism and Civil Aviation, Lok Sabha Secretariat, New Delhi.

Report of Survey of Foreign Tourist Expenditure in India—1962. Ministry of Transport and Communication, Department of Transport, Government of India, Press, 1966.

Sargent Committee Report, 1946. Ministry of Transport, Government of India, New Delhi.

Second Five Year Plan. Planning Commission, Government of India, New Delhi.

Sixth Five Year Plan. Planning Commission, Government of India, New Delhi.

Third Five Year Plan. Planning Commission, Government of India, New Delhi.

The Pattern of Tourism in India. Report of Tourist Traffic Survey, 1957, Research and Statistics Department, Department of Tourism, June, 1959.

The Future of Tourism on the Pacific and the Far East. Report prepared by Checchi & Co., under contract with the United States Department of Commerce and co-sponsored by the Pacific Area Travel Association, (PATA), 1961.

UNITED NATIONS REPORTS

Planning and Development of the Tourist Industry in the ECE Regions, Proceedings of the Symposium held at Dubrovnik (Yugoslavia) in 1975, United Nations, New York, 1976.

Report on Tourism. United Nations Development Programme, United Nations, New York.

Report on Tourism, Policy and International Tourism in OECD Member Countries. OECD, Paris, 1982.

Tourism: Sector Working Paper. World Bank, Washington DC, USA, 1972.

United Nations Conference on International Travel and Tourism. Recommendations on International Travel and Tourism,

United Nations Publication, New York, 1954.

World Travel. International Union of Official Travel Organizations, Geneva, Switzerland.

A Community Policy on Tourism, Initial Guidelines. Bulletin of the European Communities, Luxembourg, 1982.

REPORTS OF NATIONAL COUNCIL OF APPLIED ECONOMIC RESEARCH, NEW DELHI

Attitude Towards and Motivations for Savings. NCAER, New Delhi, 1964.

Cost-Benefit Study of Tourism, NCAER, New Delhi, 1975.

Techno-Economic Survey of Madhya Pradesh, NCAER, New Delhi, 1969.

ARTICLES

Abbey, James. 'Package Tour Design: A Comparative Study of Demographic and Life Style Information', *Tourism Recreation Research*, Vol. VII, No. 1, June 1982, pp. 11-6.

Alexander, L.M. 'The Impact of Tourism on the Economy of CapeCod Massachusetts', *Economic Geography*, Vol. 29, 1953, pp. 320-6.

Balchandran, M. 'The Marketing of Tourism', *Economic Times*, (Supplement), 9 May 1981, pp. 1-3.

——. 'The Public Sector in Tourism Industry', *Yojana*, (Annual Number) Vol. 25, No. 1-2, 26 January 1981, pp. 41-44.

——. 'Tourism: A Success Story', *Economic Times*, (Supplement), 10 August 1981, p. vi ; 1-3.

Blake, G.H. and R.I. Lawless, 'Algerias Tourist Industry', *Geography*, Vol. 57, April 1972, pp. 148-52.

Brook, E.B. 'Tourist Boom Petering Out!,' *Eastern Economist*, Vol. 49, No. 6, 11 August 1967, pp. 261-2.

Butler, R.W. 'The Social Implication of Tourism Development', *Tourism Research*, Vol. 2, No. 2, 1974, pp. 48-61.

Chib, S.N. 'Tourism Policy—A Political Gimmick', *Eastern Economist*, Vol. 75, No. 10, 5 Sept. 1980, pp. 548-86.

——. 'Perspectives on Indian Tourism—I', *Eastern Economist*, Vol. 77, No. 19, 6 November 1981, pp. 849-54.

——. 'Perspectives on Indian Tourism—II', *Eastern Economist*, Vol. 77, No. 20, 13 November 1981, pp. 903-09.

Chowdhary, R.K. 'Tourist Industry in India's Economic Development', *Foreign Trade Review*, Jan.-March 1973, pp. 408-19.

Christaller, W. 'Some Considerations of Tourist Locations in Europe', *Regional Science Association*, Vol. XII, 1964, pp. 95-105.

Clement, H.G. 'The Impact of Tourist Expenditure', *Development Digest*, July 1967, p. 71.

Cohen, Eric. 'Towards a Sociology of International Tourism', *Social Research*, Vol. 39, No. 1, 1972, pp. 164-82.

D'Amore, L.J. 'The Significance of Tourism in Canada', *Business Quarterly*, Vol. 41, No. 3, 1976, pp. 27-35.

Desai, Ashok. 'Economics of Tourism', *Commerce*, (Supplement), Vol. 140, No. 3595, 17 May 1980, pp. 17-20.

DeSilva, Dalton 'Growth of Tourism in South Asia', *Commerce*, Vol. 143, No. 3662, 22 August 1981, pp. 349-51.

——. 'Promoting Regional Tourism', *Commerce*, Vol. 142, No. 3651, 6 June 1981, pp. 1102.

——. 'New Dimensions in Tourist Industry', *Indian and Foreign Review*, Vol. 17. No. 12, 1 April 1980, pp. 19-20.

——. 'What ails Indian Tourism', *Eastern Economist*, Vol. 77, No. 12, 18 September 1981, pp. 553-55.

Elkan, W. 'The Relation Between Tourism and Employment in Kenya and Tanzania', *Journal of Development Studies*, Vol. 11, 1975, pp. 120-35.

Elmer, B. 'Sweden and Tourism', *Eastern Economist*, Vol. 48, No. 8, 24 February 1967, pp. 21-4.

Froster, John 'The Sociological Consequences of Tourism', *International Journal of Comparative Sociology*, Vol. 5, No. 2, 1964, pp. 217-27.

Garg, R.B.L. 'Promoting Tourism through an Integrated Approach', *Capital*, Vol. CLXVI, No. 4523, 27 July 1978, pp. 1050-52.

Gerakis, A.S. 'Effects of Exchange Rate Devaluation and Revaluations on Receipts from Tourism', *IMF Staff Paper*, XII, November, 1965, pp. 365-84.

Goffe, P. 'Development Potential of International Tourism: How Developing Nations View Tourism', *Cornell Hotel and Restaurant Administration Quarterly*, 16, 1975, pp. 24-46.

Gopal, Ajit S. 'Indian Airlines and Tourism', *Eastern Economist*, Vol. 73, No. 16, 19 October 1979, pp. 796-804.

Govind, H. 'Consolidating Data on Indian Tourism for an Integrated Approach'. *Tourism Recreation Research*, Vol. VII, No. 1, June 1982, pp. 7-10.

Gray, H. Peter 'The Balance of Payments Cost of Foreign Travel Expenditure', *Southern Economic Journal*, Vol. XXXIV, No. 1, July 1967, p. 17.

Guha, Mukul, 'Hotel Industry in Indian Tourism', *Capital*, Vol. 187, No. 467 G, 21 September 1981, pp. 9-10.

Hasan, Javid. 'American Tourist in India', *India and Foreign Review*, Vol. 17, No. 10, 1 March 1980, pp. 9-10.

Hennssey, J. 'Increasing Competition in Tourism', *Eastern Economist*, Vol. 61, No. 3, 20 July 1973, pp. 120-23.

——. 'Tourism Around the World', *Eastern Economist*, Vol. 63, No. 14, 4 October 1974, pp. 608-10.

Hunt, John D. 'Image as a Factor in Tourism Development', *Tourism-Recreation Research*, Vol. VII, No. 1, June 1982, pp. 1-6.

Jackson, R.T. 'Problems of Tourist Industry Development on the Kenyan Coast', *Geography*, Vol. 58, Jan. 1973, pp. 62-4.

Jud, G.D. 'Tourism and Economic Growth in Mexico since 1950', *Inter-American Economic Affairs*, Vol. 28, 1974, pp. 19-43.

Kohli, J.N. 'Major Tourist Attractions on South Eastern Railway', *Capital*, Vol. CLXXXI, No. 4523, 27 July 1978, pp. 1048-9.

Martin; A. 'Swiss Transport Facilities in the Service of Tourist Industry', *Swiss Industry and Trade*, No. 1, 1965, pp. 17-24.

McIntosh, R.W. 'Some Tourism Economics', *The Cornell Quarterly*, Vol. 14, No. 2, August 1973, pp. 2-4.

Medlik, S. and V.T.C. Middletone. 'The Tourist Product and its Marketing Implications', *International Tourism Quarterly*, No. 3, 19 3, pp. 28-35.

Mitchell, F. 'The Value of Tourism in East Africa', *East African Economic Review*, Vol. 2, No. 1, June 1970, pp. 1-21.

Mukherjee, S.K. 'Promoting Tourism in Eastern India through a Common Approach', *Capital*, Vol. CLXXVI, No. 4410, 22 April 1976, pp. 620-21.

Naqshband, G. 'Integration of Tourism and Environment', *Eastern Economist*, Vol. 75, No. 24, 12 December 1980, pp. 1297-300.

Narain, P. 'Making Tourism More Profitable and Commercially Oriented', *Yojana*, Vol. 27, No. 9, 16-31 May 1983, pp. 11-12 and 29.

Naylon, J. 'Tourism-Spain's Most Important Industry', *Geography*, Vol. 52, January 1967, pp. 23-40.

Oberio, S.S. 'Role of Travel Agents in the Promotion of Tourism', *Capital*, Vol. CLXXXI, No. 4523, 27 July 1978, pp. 1052-4.

Ojha, J.M. 'Selling Benign Tourism: Case References from Indian Scene', *Tourism Recreation Research*, Vol. VII, No. 1, June 1982, pp. 23-4.

O'Loughlin, Carleen. 'Tourism in the Tropics : Lessons from the West Indies', *Insight and Opinion*, Vol. 5, No. 2, 1970, pp. 105-15.

Peaker, A. 'Holiday Spending by the British at Home and Abroad', *National Westminster Bank Quarterly Review*, August 1973, pp. 47-55.

Rai, H.L. and K.C. Rao, 'Tourism: A Boon', *Indian Journal of Marketing*, Vol. XI, No. 9, May 1981, pp. 17-19 and 32.

Ramchandran, M.G. 'Tamil Nadu: A Tourist's Paradise', *Eastern Economist*, Vol. 75, No. 24, 12 December 1980, pp. 1310-13.

Ram Lall, 'Himachal Tourism Forges Ahead', *Eastern Economist*, Vol. 75, No. 24, 12 December 1980, pp. 1314-17.

Richards, G. 'How Important is Tourism in Real Terms ?', *Catering Times*, 3 August 1972.

Robinson, G.W.S. 'The Recreation Geography of South Asia', *Geographical Review*, October 1972, pp. 561-72.

Roy, A.M. 'Bridging the Information Gap for Attracting Foreign Tourists', *Capital*, Vol. CLXV, No. 4137, 5 November 1970, pp. 793-5.

Sarkar, G. 'Growth of Air Transport will Facilitate Tourism', *Capital*, 29 June 1967, pp. 79-81.

Sharma, D.S. 'How Banks Can Help Tourism', *The Banker*, Vol. XXVI, No. 6, August 1978, pp. 11-3.

Shrivastava, K.K. 'Tourism in India', *Yojana*, Vol. 27, No. 10, 1-15 June 1983, pp. 7-9.

Srinivasa, Raghavan, T.C.A. '3.5 Million Tourists? Where will they Stay?', *Eastern Economist*, Vol. 75, No. 24, 12 December 1980, pp. 1308-10.

Sundaresan, M. 'Rapid Growth of Tourism', *Commerce*, Vol. 137, No. 3516, 28 October 1978, pp. 1-5.

Sutton, W.A. 'Travel and Understanding: Notes on the Social Structure of Touring', *International Journal of Comparative Sociology*, Vol. 8, No. 2, 1967, pp. 218-23.

Tambay, Vaidya Malati. 'Role of State Government in Promotion of Tourism', *Commerce*, Vol. 137, No. 3516, 28 October, 1978, pp. 8-9.

——. 'Tourism in Maharashtra—Economic Aspects', *Eastern Economist*, Vol. 73, No. 16, 19 October 1979, pp. 808-12.

Tata, J.R.D. 'The Story of Indian Air Transport', *Journal of Royal Aeronautical Society*, London, 1961.

——. 'Trends in Air Transportations', *Eastern Economist*, Vol. 70, No. 12, 24 March 1978, pp. 596-600.

Thuens, H.L. 'Notes on the Economics of International Tourism in Developing Countries', *Tourist Review*, Vol. 31 (3), 1976, pp. 2-10.

Ummat, R.C. 'Fostering Tourism—Why dither?', *Eastern Economist*, Vol. 73, No. 16, 19 October 1979, pp. 796-804.

Uvalic, Radivoj. 'Yogoslavia in International Tourist Year', *Eastern Economist*, Vol. 48, No. 8, 24 February 1967, pp. 14-8.

Venu, S. 'Economics of Tourism', *Eastern Economist*, Vol. 58, No. 16, 9 June 1972, pp. 1127-29.

Wilson, P. 'Indian Tourism—Image in the Minds of Foreign Tourists', *Indian Journal of Marketing*, Vol. X, No. 12, August 1980, pp. 3-8.

——. 'Problems of Promotion of Tourism', *Eastern Economist*, Vol. 75, No. 24, 12 December 1980, pp. 1301-04.

Wilson, P. 'Implications of Tourism in India', *Indian Journal of Marketing*, Vol. XI, No. 4, December 1980, pp. 7-10.

MISCELLANEOUS

Craig, Paul G. 'The Future Growth of Hawaiian Tourism and Its Impact on the Neighbour Islands', Ph.D. Thesis, Economic Research Centre, University of Hawaii, 1963.

Economic Impact of Recreation, Vacation and Travel on New Hampshire. Division of Economic Development, State of New Hampshire, 1962.

Gorra, Pierre. *Nouvelle etude prospective sur l'apport du tourisme au developpement economique du Liban,* Department Researches et Documentation, O.N.T., Lebanon, 1967.

Master Plan for the Developement of Tourism in Pakistan, 1965.

Suits, Daniel B. *An Econometric Model of the Greek Economy,* Centre of Economic Research, Athens, 1964.

Study of the Economics of Tourism in Ireland, 1966.

Inedx